# CONTRACT
# WITH AMERICA

# CONTRACT
# WITH AMERICA

*The Bold Plan by*
*Rep. Newt Gingrich, Rep. Dick Armey*
*and the House Republicans*
*to Change the Nation*

EDITED BY ED GILLESPIE AND BOB SCHELLHAS

TIMES 𝕿 BOOKS

RANDOM HOUSE

*Publisher's Note:*
*Neither Rep. Newt Gingrich, Rep. Dick Armey,*
*nor any House Republican received (or will receive)*
*any compensation for the publication of* Contract
with America. *Royalties from the sale of this*
*document will be used for nonpolitical, nonpartisan purposes.*

All rights reserved under International and Pan-American
Copyright Conventions. Published in the United States by Times Books,
a division of Random House, Inc., New York, and simultaneously
in Canada by Random House of Canada Limited, Toronto.

ISBN: 0-8129-2586-6

Manufactured in the United States of America

9 8 7 6 5 4 3 2

First Edition

# Contents

# *Acknowledgments*

*Contract with America* was the final product of the work of a great many talented people. The 367 Republican candidates who signed their names on the dotted line to help change the nation, should be recognized for accepting the responsibility of putting forward a bold agenda.

Dozens of House Republicans in eleven working groups worked tirelessly under tight deadlines to draft the ten bills that make up the heart of this book. The members of Congress who headed these working groups deserve credit for moving ideas into legislation. We would like to thank Reps. Jennifer Dunn of Washington and David Dreier of California for the opening-day checklist; Reps. Jim Saxton of New Jersey and Tom DeLay of Texas for the Job Creation and Wage Enhancement Act; Rep. Lamar Smith of Texas for the Fiscal Responsibility Act; Reps. Dave Camp of Michigan and Jim Talent of Missouri for the Personal Responsibility Act; Rep. Bill McCollum of Florida for the Taking Back Our Streets Act; Rep. John Linder of Georgia for the Citizen Legislature Act; Reps. Henry Hyde of Illinois and Barbara Vucanovich for the Family Reinforcement Act and the American Dream Restoration Act; Rep. Dennis Hastert of Illinois for the Senior Citizen Equity Act; Rep. Jim Ramstad of Minnesota for the Common Sense Legal Reform Act; and Rep. Bob Livingston of Louisiana for the National Security Restoration Act. In addition, we thank Bill Gribbin, staff member of the policy committee who helped develop the ten bills.

Another key group of members of Congress dedicated a great amount of time and energy in planning the overall strategy for *Contract with America*: Rep. John Boehner of Ohio; Rep. Jim Nussle of Iowa; Rep. Deborah Pryce of Ohio; Rep. Peter Hoekstra of Michigan; Dan Meyer, chief of staff to Rep. Newt Gingrich, Tony Blankley, spokesman to Rep. Newt Gingrich, and Jerry Climer of the Congressional Institute.

Of course, members of Congress rely heavily on staff to implement their ideas. The staff of the House Republican Conference played a key role in bringing together the bills in the *Contract with America* and the September 27, 1994, event in Washington, D.C., to unveil it. They are Peter Davidson, Ginni Thomas, Brian Gaston, Brenda Benjamin, Carie Stephens, Mary Catherine English, Siobhan McGill, and Ed Gillespie (who co-edited this book). The staff of the *Legislative Digest* prepared detailed descriptions of each of the bills for the public, much of which appears in this book. They are Stacy Shrader, Jim Wilkinson, Katie Podlesak, Alice Anne English, and Brian Fortune. As always, John Sampson, editor of the *Digest*, did an outstanding job bringing everything together.

The *Contract* would not have had nearly the impact it did if not for the generosity of Republican National Committee Chairman Haley Barbour and the talents of his staff, especially RNC Executive Director Scott Reed, Communications Director Chuck Greener, Leigh Ann Metzger, Paula Nowakowski and the entire communications division, Research Director Dan

Casey, and Director of Strategic Planning and Congressional Affairs Don Fierce. A party chief with vision, Haley agreed that we should not only run against something or someone but should restate what it is the GOP stands for. He dedicated people and resources to the success of the project. Chief among the people dedicated was Barry Jackson, who was Director of the *Contract with America* office at the Republican National Committee. The staff included Deputy Director Bob Schellhas (who co-edited this book), Mike Donohue, Patrick Dougherty, Brady Newby, Ruth Guimond, and Judy Biviano. Countless volunteers, especially House Republican press secretaries, gave much of their personal time to this effort.

Rep. Bill Paxon of New York, chairman of the National Republican Congressional Committee, shared our commitment to a positive policy agenda, and his staff, notably Executive Director Maria Cino and Communications Director Dan Leonard, provided critical support to the project as well. A special thanks is owed to the following for their tactical support: Barrie Tron, Keith Apel, Greg Mueller, Michael Deaver, Rob Rehg, and Jim Hooley.

We save the most important staff person for last. Kerry A. Knott, executive director of the House Republican Conference, carried the burden of this project from inception to completion. The first to identify the ten bills as a "contract," he worked tirelessly for months on what was his raison d'etre. Without his complete dedication, *Contract with America* would simply not have been accomplished.

# CONTRACT WITH AMERICA

# Contract with America

ELECTION DAY, November 8, 1994, was a turning point. America's voters dismantled the forty-year lock the Democrats had on Congress, giving Republicans control of the U.S. Senate and the U.S. House of Representatives. For the first time in more than 130 years, a sitting Speaker of the House was defeated for reelection. And despite their ability to wield influence inside the Washington Beltway, two of the most powerful committee chairmen in the House were dethroned by the voters back home.

Voters sent a clear, undeniable message. It wasn't just about throwing out incumbents, it was about throwing out Democrats. Incredibly, not a single incumbent Republican congressman, senator, or governor was defeated. For the first time in more than twenty years, Republicans gained a majority of the nation's governorships and picked up control of seventeen more state legislative chambers. Obviously the voters believed there was a difference between the way the two parties envisioned the role of government in their lives, and the difference mattered.

Nothing written before or after the election better defines the difference between the two parties than the document you now hold in your hands—the *Contract with America*. Rarely has such a meaningful mandate for change been delivered by voters. That mandate is articulated in the common-sense agenda of the *Con-*

*tract*, the essence of which was presented by Republican candidates six weeks before voters went to the polls and has been much discussed ever since. For the first time in memory, American citizens have a document they can refer to as a means of holding Congress accountable. Returning accountability, and the faith and trust that come with it, was the very reason for creating this *Contract*.

The notion for such a contract was born on a snowy weekend in February 1994, if not by a word then by deed. At a conference of House Republicans in Salisbury, Maryland, a direction was set for making sure citizens could clearly understand what the Republican Party stood for and meant to deliver if ever given a chance to control the federal legislative process. It was clear to us that after a year in the White House, President Bill Clinton did not intend to govern on the agenda which people elected him to lead the country. At the Salisbury conference, House Republicans talked about governing the country with the will of the people in the U.S. House of Representatives. They understood the need to articulate a clear vision of what they stood for and what direction they would take the country. From these discussions, they agreed upon five principles to describe their basic philosophy of American civilization:

—**individual liberty**
—**economic opportunity**
—**limited government**
—**personal responsibility**
—**security at home and abroad.**

Based upon these principles House Republicans outlined a vision for America's future and the role of government. That vision seeks to renew the American Dream by promoting individual liberty, economic opportunity, and personal responsibility, through limited and effective government, high standards of performance, and an America strong enough to defend all her citizens against violence at home or abroad.

The principles and vision developed by House Republicans determined our mission—a mission of working together to offer representative governance, and to communicate our vision of America through clearly defined themes, programs and legislative initiatives to earn us the honor of becoming the majority party in 1995.

*Contract with America* evolved from the Salisbury conference and was an effort to accomplish the mission as defined by House Republicans. They recognized the need to restore the fabric of trust between the American people and their officeholders. Public confidence in Congress and other institutions had reached its lowest point in twenty years. The feeling among voters that elected officials are not accountable to the same rules as everyone else and do not understand their frustration with a political process that doesn't work for them had to be addressed. *Contract with America* was an instrument to help repair a fundamental disconnection between citizens and their elected officials.

Since the early spring of 1994, House Republican members and candidates worked together, listening to citizens, in developing the legislative proposals that would form the foundation of the *Contract*. The result was a bold agenda that offers real change. It forces the House of Representatives to operate under the same rules and budget constraints as businesses and households do. It proposes ten specific pieces of legislation to limit and hold government accountable; to promote economic opportunity and individual responsibility for families and businesses; and to maintain security both at home and abroad.

The *Contract* was unveiled to the public on September 27, 1994, when more than 300 Republican candidates for the U.S. House of Representatives stood on the West Front of the U.S. Capitol under an unusually warm, sun-filled sky to make history. They made the journey to Washington, D.C., from as far as Hawaii and from as near as Northern Virginia on the opposite bank of the Potomac River. All told, 367 candidates signed the *Contract with America* to bring fundamental change to the way business is done in the people's House of Representatives, and to give rebirth to an open political process that provides substantive debates and votes upon issues of common agreement among the vast majority of Americans.

The candidates who signed on the dotted line carry a responsibility to do what they can to make the principles of the *Contract* a reality. *Contract with America* is an agreement and a covenant between our now elected representatives and the American people with whom we sought a common bond. As the newly elected majority in the House of Representatives, Republicans have a blueprint for action.

On January 4, 1995, as the 104th Congress is sworn in to support and defend the Constitution, the new Republican House majority will begin to deliver on the *Contract* they signed and sealed with the American people.

Here is the pact that was signed on September 27, 1994, and which we pledge to honor:

## CONTRACT WITH AMERICA

As Republican Members of the House of Representatives and as citizens seeking to join that body we propose not just to change its policies, but even more important, to restore the bonds of trust between the people and their elected representatives. That is why, in this era of official evasion and posturing, we offer instead a detailed agenda for national renewal, a written commitment with no fine print.

This year's election offers the chance, after four decades of one-party control, to bring to the House a new majority that will transform the way Congress works. That historic change would be the end of government that is too big, too intrusive, and too easy with the public's money. It can be the beginning of a Congress that respects the values and shares the faith of the American family.

Like Lincoln, our first Republican president, we intend to act "with firmness in the right, as God gives us to see the right." To restore accountability to Congress. To end its cycle of scandal and disgrace. To make us all proud again of the way free people govern themselves.

On the first day of the 104th Congress, the new Republican majority will immediately pass the following major reforms, aimed at restoring the faith and trust of the American people in their government:

*First*, require all laws that apply to the rest of the country also apply equally to the Congress;

*Second*, select a major independent auditing firm to conduct a comprehensive audit of Congress for waste, fraud, or abuse;

*Third*, cut the number of House committees, and cut committee staff by one-third;

*Fourth*, limit the terms of all committee chairs;

*Fifth*, ban the casting of proxy votes in committee;

*Sixth*, require committee meetings to be open to the public;

*Seventh*, require a three-fifths majority vote to pass a tax increase;

*Eighth*, guarantee an honest accounting of our federal budget by implementing zero baseline budgeting.

Thereafter, within the first hundred days of the 104th Congress, we shall bring to the House Floor the following bills, each to be given full and open debate, each to be given a clear and fair vote, and each to be immediately available this day for public inspection and scrutiny.

### The Fiscal Responsibility Act

• A balanced budget/tax limitation amendment and a legislative line-item veto to restore fiscal responsibility to an out-of-control Congress, requiring them to live under the same budget constraints as families and businesses.

### The Taking Back Our Streets Act

• An anti-crime package including stronger truth in sentencing, "good faith" exclusionary rule exemptions, effective death penalty provisions, and cuts in social spending from this summer's crime bill to fund prison construction and additional law enforcement to keep people secure in their neighborhoods and kids safe in their schools.

### The Personal Responsibility Act

• Discourage illegitimacy and teen pregnancy by prohibiting welfare to minor mothers and denying increased AFDC for additional children while on welfare, cut spending for welfare programs, and enact a tough two-years-and-out provision with work requirements to promote individual responsibility.

### The Family Reinforcement Act

• Child support enforcement, tax incentives for adoption, strengthening rights of parents in their children's education, stronger child pornography laws, and an elderly dependent care tax credit to reinforce the central role of families in American society.

### The American Dream Restoration Act

• A $500-per-child tax credit, begin repeal of the marriage tax penalty, and creation of American Dream Savings Accounts to provide middle-class tax relief.

### The National Security Restoration Act

• No U.S. troops under UN command and restoration of the essential parts of our national security funding to strengthen our national defense and maintain our credibility around the world.

### The Senior Citizens Fairness Act

• Raise the Social Security earnings limit, which currently forces seniors out of the workforce, repeal the 1993 tax hikes on Social Security benefits, and provide tax incentives for private long-term care insurance to let older Americans keep more of what they have earned over the years.

## The Job Creation and Wage Enhancement Act

• Small business incentives, capital gains cut and indexation, neutral cost recovery, risk assessment/cost-benefit analysis, strengthening of the Regulatory Flexibility Act and unfunded mandate reform to create jobs and raise worker wages.

## The Common Sense Legal Reforms Act

• "Loser pays" laws, reasonable limits on punitive damages, and reform of product liability laws to stem the endless tide of litigation.

## The Citizen Legislature Act

• A first-ever vote on term limits to replace career politicians with citizen legislators.

Further, we will instruct the House Budget Committee to report to the floor and we will work to enact additional budget savings, beyond the budget cuts specifically included in the legislation described above, to ensure that the federal budget deficit will be less than it would have been without the enactment of these bills.

Respecting the judgment of our fellow citizens as we seek their mandate for reform, we hereby pledge our names to this *Contract with America*. (All the names of the signatories to the *Contract* can be found in the Appendix.)

Standing up against the Clinton administration's tax-and-spend assault on American families was worth a great deal to Republicans in the November elections, but standing up for a positive agenda to help restore the American dream and the integrity of government was worth a lot more. The more than 300 Republican House candidates who stood on the steps of the U.S. Capitol and signed a contract with America laid out the ten bills Americans would see within the first hundred days of the first Republican-controlled House of Representatives in four decades.

A week later, on October 4, Republican candidates for state legislatures stood on the steps of state capitols across the country and made similar commitments to the people of their states. On October 11, local candidates stood before their county courthouses and city halls to seal similar contracts with voters. These events marked a defining moment for Republicans in the midterm elections.

Like it or not, the Republican Party in 1992 was largely defined by the Clinton campaign, and our misbegotten identity as the party of the rich and out-of-touch is still not far from the average voter's mind. The September 27, 1994, U.S. Capitol event and subsequent state and local versions were an opportunity to reclaim our mantle as the party of the middle class, the party of reform, and the party that values individual freedom and individual responsibility over government power and government responsibility.

Sadly, it is difficult today for either party or any candidate to penetrate the shell of cynicism encasing voters today. As far as many Americans are concerned, campaign promises are not worth much because politicians too often forget them as soon as they are made. To rebuild the faith that is needed for representative government to really work, it was necessary to produce a signed, written contract that states explicitly, "If we break the contract, throw us out."

The *Contract with America* is an opportunity to restore the American dream with creative legislative solutions. At the same time, it will restore the bonds of trust between the people and their elected representatives, making us proud once again of the way free people govern themselves.

### Forty Years Was Long Enough

The Democrats' iron-handed, one-party rule of the House of Representatives over the last four decades led to arcane, arbitrary, and often secretive procedures that disenfranchised millions of Americans from representation in Congress. This autocratic rule was a direct attack on the free democratic principles upon which our nation was founded. The result was a Congress held in contempt not only for failing to act on crucial issues but also for holding itself above the law and operating in secret. Congress simply could not change until the party in charge of Congress changed.

*Contract with America* is rooted in three core principles:

## *Accountability*

• Elected officials have become so entrenched and protected that they are unresponsive to the public they were elected to serve. We must make government more efficient, making sure taxpayers get their money's worth and wresting power from special interest groups and returning it to the public. Our contract includes a number of substantive reforms to restore accountability to a government that's grown larger than ever imagined by our Founding Fathers.

## *Responsibility*

• The Clinton Congress defaulted on its proper responsibility for protecting the citizenry. It mistook a responsibility to protect the public from violent crime for an opportunity to spend billions more on social programs. But Big Brother is alive and well through myriad government programs usurping personal responsibility from families and individuals. Meanwhile, our judicial system saps our nation's productivity and encourages frivolous "get-rich-quick" lawsuits. Our contract seeks to restore a proper balance between government and personal responsibility.

## *Opportunity*

• Republicans want to restore the opportunity for all Americans to achieve the American dream, which now exceeds the grasp of too many families. Burdensome government regulations stifle wages, economic growth levels are frustratingly below the post–World War II norm, and the average family today spends more on taxes than it spends on food, clothing, and shelter combined. The result is that middle-class families are making their first home purchase later in life, scrambling to pay college tuition, and putting a second earner in the market not to support the household but to support the cost of government.

## Ten Bills in a Hundred Days

The *Contract* represents a dramatic change in direction for federal policymaking. The pace of ten major bills in the first hundred days indicates the magnitude of change to come. The bills include a first-ever vote on congressional term limits, a balanced budget amendment, welfare reform, tax cuts for families, and strong national defense measures.

## Opening-Day Checklist

The very first day of a Republican House will bring marked change to the business as usual seen in the House of Representatives since 1954. As part of an opening-day checklist, the new Republican leadership will:

- Apply all laws to Congress.

- Cut the number of committees and subcommittees, and cut committee staffs by a third.

- Limit the terms of committee chairs and ranking members.

- Ban "proxy" (ghost) voting in committee.

- Implement an "honest numbers" budget with a zero baseline.

- Require committee meetings to be open to the public.

- Require a three-fifths majority to pass a tax increase.

- Audit the House's books with an independent firm.

After changing the way the House does business, Republicans will change the business the House does. Instead of passing bills that pile taxes, spending, and regulations ever higher, we'll scale back government to make it more efficient and ease the burden on taxpayers and small business people.

### Ten Bills: Signed Promises, Specific Goals

1. *Balanced budget amendment/line-item veto.*

2. *Stop violent criminals:*
   —effective death penalty provisions;
   —greater emphasis on prison funding and law enforcement.

3. *Welfare reform:*
   —discourages illegitimacy and teen pregnancy by prohibiting welfare to minor mothers and denying increased AFDC for additional children while on welfare;
   —cuts spending for welfare programs;
   —ends welfare for families collecting AFDC for five years and for noncitizens;
   —requires welfare recipients to work.

4. *Protect our kids:*
   —child support enforcement;
   —tax incentives for adoption;
   —strengthening rights of parents in their children's education;
   —stronger child pornography laws;
   —an elderly dependent care tax credit.

5. *Tax cuts for families:*
   —a $500-per-child family tax credit;
   —reforming the anti-marriage bias in the tax code;
   —an "American Dream Savings Accounts" in the form of individual retirement accounts (IRAs) for first-time home buyers, education expenses, and retirement.

6. *Strong national defense:*
   —no U.S. troops under UN command;

—building budget firewalls between defense and nondefense spending to prevent raids on the defense budget;
—creating a missile defense system against rogue dictatorships like North Korea.

7. *Raise the senior citizens' earning limit:*
—increases the earnings limit to at least $30,000;
—repeals the Clinton tax hikes on Social Security benefits;
—provides tax incentives for private long-term care insurance.

8. *Economic growth and regulatory reform:*
—capital gains cut and indexation;
—neutral cost recovery;
—risk assessment/cost-benefit analysis;
—strengthening the Regulatory Flexibility Act;
—unfunded mandates reforms.

9. *Common sense legal reforms:*
—"loser pays" to stop frivolous lawsuits;
—limits on punitive damages;
—honesty in evidence to exclude "junk science."

10. *Congressional term limits:*
—a first-ever vote on term limits for members of Congress to replace career politicians with citizen legislators,

including six-year and twelve-year term limits.

## *From the U.S. Capitol to the State Capitols*

One week after these reforms were unveiled on the steps of the U.S. Capitol, state legislators and candidates took to the steps of state capitols across the country to present their contracts to state voters, and a week after that local candidates stood on the steps of city hall to put in writing their commitment to lower taxes, personal freedom and responsibility, and government accountability.

Many of the bills promised in the first hundred days of the Republican House of Representatives may seem familiar to state legislators, because they bubbled up from the state level. In fact, innovative ideas like "three-strikes-and-you're-out" anti-crime measures, tax limitation measures, work over welfare measures, and health care insurance reforms have come from state legislatures or statewide voter referendums.

Among the issues Republican state candidates emphasized:

• State insurance reforms that would enable people to change jobs without losing health care coverage because of a pre-existing condition, thus eliminating the middle-class phenomenon of "job lock."

• Line-item veto authority for governors in those states without this crucial check on government spending.

- Ending traditional cash benefits for able-bodied welfare recipients, and replacing them with support that offers real hope and opportunity like day care, child support from absent fathers, and support for work efforts without creating a culture of long-term dependency.

At the local level, innovative Republican mayors such as Jersey City's Bret Schundler and Indianapolis's Steve Goldsmith are breaking the molds of city governments. While holding the line on taxes, Republican mayors are making the delivery of local services more efficient through privatization, education choice, and other reforms that inject fresh thinking into municipal government. Reforms like these, combined with relief from unfunded federal mandates, will make state and local governments more responsive to the needs of their constituents and more efficient in delivering services.

It's significant and telling that it was only after losing the White House for the first time in twelve years that Republicans were able to capture the mayoralties of America's biggest cities, New York and Los Angeles. And now the voters have once again voiced their concerns and their issues at the ballot box by entrusting Republicans with control of the House of Representatives.

The bold initiatives we're talking about in the specific language of actual legislation represents one of the most dramatic comebacks in American politics. A scant twenty months after losing the White House and reading the rumors of our party's death in newspapers across the country, our candidates were more energized and our party was more unified than we could have dared to hope. We have not only Bill Clinton to thank for that but, as our *Contract with America* shows throughout the following pages, the creative thinkers in our party at all levels of government.

The belief that you can trust Americans to make valid judgments permeates Republican initiatives from the smallest hamlet to the halls of the U.S. Congress. Whether it's $500 more in the pockets of parents, the prerogative to choose their children's schools, the right to express opinions through initiative and referendum, or reining in the bureaucratic trampling of private property rights, Republican legislators recognize the innate ability of every American to make decisions around the kitchen table without some dictum handed down from Washington.

*Contract with America*, as ambitious as it is, is only the agenda of the first hundred days of the first Republican-controlled House of Representatives in more than four decades. It represents the first substantive steps on the road to a smaller government with lower taxes and fewer regulations.

Republicans promise to bring these bills to the floor of the House of Representatives for a fair and honest debate, but part of the responsibility for their passage rests with the American people. In a Republican House, it will be easier for the public to obtain information (all the bills in the *Contract with America* are currently on the Internet system) and have their views represented (we pledge to allow more amendments). That provides people greater opportunity for participating in the legislative process.

This book makes available to you in great detail the provisions we have pledged to carry out. Whether you agree or disagree with any or all of the bills that make up the *Contract with America*, please make your voice heard. We made a point of letting the people know where we stood on these important issues, and now it is up to you to let your representative know where you stand on them.

The debate over the direction of our government, between smaller government with lower taxes and fewer services or bigger government with higher taxes and more services, affects every American. Passage of the *Contract* will dramatically change the way Washington does business, and change the business Washington does. In two years, the public will have a record to look at, and they will know whether Republicans really were different when they took control of the people's House for the first time in forty years, or if they slipped easily into business as usual. If we live up to the *Contract*, and reform Congress, the people will give us the honor of continuing to serve in the majority. If we fail, we know we will be shown the door in much the same way the Democrats were in this past election.

# Balanced Budget Amendment and Line-Item Veto

IsN'T IT TIME we hold Congress accountable for how much they spend—and for what? The American people demand responsibility from Congress. The spending madness must stop. Our *Contract with America* begins with fiscal responsibility. Just as every American sits at the kitchen table and balances his or her budget, just as every small business must balance its budget, Congress must begin balancing our nation's budget—now. That's why in the first hundred days of a Republican House we will vote on the Fiscal Responsibility Act.

Our *Contract with America* calls for a balanced budget amendment to the Constitution. And to keep Congress from passing the bill to you, our balanced budget amendment requires a three-fifths majority of Congress to raise taxes. And to increase accountability for the budget, our *Contract* calls for a line-item veto, to give the President—Republican or Democrat—the authority to cut wasteful pork-barrel spending.

Balancing the budget will not be easy. It will require a fundamental restructuring of government. We believe the American people are ready for government that does less of the wrong things, but does the right things well. The balanced budget amendment is supported by 80 percent of the American people. Just as the ruling Democrats in Congress ignored the people on most issues, it ignored them on spending as well. By twisting arms to block the balanced budget amendment, the Democratic Party protected its irresponsible tax-and-spend policies that weakened this great nation.

With the help of the American people, we will put our fiscal house in order.

## The Fiscal Responsibility Act

Controlling spending is the primary means to controlling the deficit. Republicans favor institutional reforms that would pressure Congress to cut spending. Regrettably, the White House and the Democratic congressional majority, whose power depended on the ability to deliver huge spending projects, have in the past blocked such institutional reform. Indeed, Democrats in Congress have an overall record of voting for spending bills twice as often as Republicans. The Fiscal Responsibility Act we propose contains two powerful, common sense ways to control Congress's penchant for spending:

• A balanced budget amendment to the Constitution with a tax limitation provision, which requires a three-fifths vote by both the House and Senate to raise taxes.

• In order to regain control over spending, the Fiscal Responsibility Act gives the President a permanent line-item veto. The bill calls for an up-or-down vote on the President's package of rescissions, and the cuts would automatically become effective unless

Congress rejects them. If Congress rejects the package, the President can veto the rejection, and a two-thirds vote would be required to overturn it.

Congress has shown itself both unwilling and incapable of balancing the federal budget. A constitutional amendment is necessary to force lawmakers to do what on their own they cannot: get a handle on out-of-control spending. Opponents of the idea argue it will transfer budget decision making to the courts, will result in massive cuts in Social Security, and will usurp Congress's constitutional authority to control government purse strings.

Given our current deficit situation, the President should have line-item veto authority to single out unnecessary and wasteful spending provisions in bills passed by Congress. Many critics assert, however, that the line-item veto will give too much power to the executive branch to control federal spending—a responsibility clearly given to the legislative branch in the U.S. Constitution.

## Background

Perpetual annual deficits, compounded by the fact that the federal government has not ended a fiscal year in surplus since 1969, has led many economists, former presidents, members of Congress and the public at large to call for more stringent and binding budget mechanisms—mechanisms that Congress will not be able to routinely waive or ignore. Many Americans have become disillusioned with a Congress that has consistently found ways to circumvent the few budgetary restraints it has set for itself:

- In 1985, Congress passed the Balanced Budget and Emergency Deficit Control Act (popularly known as Gramm-Rudman-Hollings) to establish steadily declining deficit targets, supposedly bringing a balanced budget in FY 1991. In September 1987, faced with a projected budget deficit of $183 billion for FY 1988 (far exceeding the $108 billion target), Congress revised the law and adopted higher deficit levels supposedly bringing a balanced budget in FY 1993. In 1990, and again in 1993, Congress revised and extended these targets—postponing a balanced budget indefinitely.

- Congressional budget rules allow the House of Representatives to automatically raise the ceiling on the federal debt without a separate vote—protecting individual members of Congress from the difficult decision of increasing the federal debt.

These and other actions demonstrate to many that Congress has neither the will nor the desire to cut wasteful government spending and pass into law a balanced budget.

### The Balanced Budget Amendment's Recent History

In addition to the line-item veto, one of the more rigorous proposals that has garnered significant popular and Congressional support is the balanced budget amendment. A June 11, 1992, *Investors' Business Daily* article cited a *Washington Post*/ABC News poll finding that 75 percent of Americans favor a balanced budget amendment. However, Congress has been considering balanced budget amendments since 1936 with little success. The closest Congress ever came to passing one was in 1986, when the Senate defeated a balanced budget resolution by one vote.

The House last considered a balanced budget amendment in March 1994. At that time, four different versions of the amendment were debated. The first would have amended the U.S. Constitution to require that total outlays for any fiscal year not exceed total receipts for that year unless three-fifths of the House and three-fifths of the Senate vote to incur a deficit. The authors made an exception for any fiscal year in which a declaration of war is in effect or the United States is engaged in a military conflict that poses a threat to national security. The proposal also required (1) a three-fifths roll call vote in each chamber to increase the public debt limit and (2) that a majority of the membership of each chamber approve a tax increase. On final passage, it failed 271–153 — 12 votes shy of the two-thirds margin.

The House also rejected a substitute version giving the President the line-item veto, limiting outlays to 19 percent of GDP for a given fiscal year, and requiring a three-fifths vote in both chambers to waive the requirement, and another substitute allowing a majority of the House and Senate to waive the balanced budget requirement in times of war, military conflict, or economic recession and exempting Social Security. Although the House adopted an amendment requiring three-fifths roll-call votes of the total membership of the House and Senate or a declaration of war to waive the balanced budget amendment, and a three-fifths vote to increase the debt limit or raise taxes, it was not considered to be finally adopted since the substitutes were considered under king-of-the-hill procedures (i.e., the last amendment adopted in the Committee of the Whole is reported back the House for a vote on final passage). Because the first version of the amendment was considered and passed after passage of the last proposed amendment, only the former was considered to have been adopted in the Committee of the Whole. Thus, only it was reported back to the House, where it failed to receive the necessary two-thirds vote.

A few weeks prior to House consideration of the balanced budget amendment, the Senate debated a similar resolution, rejecting it on March 1, 1994, by a vote of 63–37—four votes short of the required two-thirds margin. That measure, sponsored by Democratic Senator Paul Simon, would have made the balanced budget requirement effective two years after its ratification or in 2002, whichever came later. During consideration, the Senate also rejected an alternative resolution ensuring (1) that courts cannot impose tax hikes if Congress fails to balance the budget, (2) exempting Social Security, (3) allowing Congress to waive the balanced budget requirement in times of economic recession, and (4) permitting the government to borrow for infrastructure needs. It was defeated 22–78.

## Amendments to the Constitution

As stipulated in the U.S. Constitution, amendments to our founding document must be approved by two-thirds of those present and voting in both the House and Senate and three-fourths (38) of the fifty state legislatures. The Constitution has been amended twenty-seven times, including amendments protecting the free exercise of religion; protecting the right to keep and bear arms; protecting against unreasonable searches and seizures; guaranteeing the right to a speedy and public trial; protecting against cruel and unusual punishment; abolishing slavery; guaranteeing equal protection under the law to all; giving Congress the power to tax; prohibiting the manufacture, sale, or transportation of alcohol and then later repealing this prohibition; and giving women the right to vote. The most recent constitutional amendment—prohibiting a congressional pay raise from taking effect during the Congress in which it was adopted—was ratified on May 7, 1992.

## Line-Item Veto

A rescission bill rescinds or cancels, in whole or part, spending previously authorized by Congress to reduce spending or eliminate the spending because it is no longer needed. Under current law, rescissions proposed by the President must be transmitted in a special message to Congress. Under the 1974 Impoundment Control Act, Congress must complete action on a rescission bill within forty-five days of continuous session after receipt of the proposal or else the authorized spending must be made available.

Budget rules governing rescissions stipulate that if the Appropriations Committee does not act on rescissions submitted by the President within twenty-five days of continuous session, one-fifth of the members of the House of Representatives can call for discharge of the bill from committee. (House rules for other bills require a waiting period of thirty days and that a majority of members sign a discharge petition.)

The Impoundment Control Act of 1974 was the congressional response to the Nixon administration's fondness for rescinding or deferring budget authority previously approved by Congress. This confrontation intensified in the 92nd and 93rd Congresses as President Nixon used the impoundment tool to reorder national priorities and alter programs supported by lawmakers. In the Act, Congress required the President to inform it of all proposed rescissions and deferrals and submit specific information regarding each proposal. The original provisions of the Act allowed a deferral to take effect unless either the House or the Senate took action to disapprove it—effectively providing for a one-house veto. This procedure was invalidated by the 1983 Supreme Court decision in *INS v. Chadha*. In 1986, a federal district court ruled that the President's deferral authority under the act was no longer available, since it was inextricably linked to the one-house veto provision in the law. The lower court decision was upheld by the appeals court in 1987. Congress responded to these rulings with the Balanced Budget Affirmation Act, which did away with policy-based deferrals and amended the original act to comply with the court's decision.

The current debate on presidential authority arises out of the fact that presidents can veto appropriations bills in their entirety, but not in part. Supporters of the line-item veto argue that the President should be able to selectively weed out wasteful pork-barrel spending in an otherwise good bill. In the 103rd Congress over twenty line-item veto bills were introduced. The House twice passed so-called expedited rescissions legislation, which require presidential rescissions to be approved by Congress under accelerated committee and floor procedures. However, they were never considered by the Democratic-controlled Senate. Another version of the line-item veto, considered as an amendment to these bills, is the "enhanced rescission" proposal, which forces Congress to pass a disapproval bill to block proposed presidential cuts. A constitutional line-item veto or a stand-alone legislative line-item veto has never been considered by the House—all line-item veto proposals have been considered as amendments to other bills, and have either failed or been dropped from the final version of the legislation. Forty-three of the nation's governors have a line-item veto authority of some sort.

Here's what our *Contract with America* proposes:

## Balanced Budget Amendment

The Fiscal Responsibility Act amends the U.S. Constitution to require that total outlays for any fiscal year do not exceed total receipts for that year. The resolution defines *receipts* as all receipts except those derived from borrowing, and *outlays* as all outlays except principal payments on the debt. It requires that the President submit, and Congress pass, a balanced budget each fiscal year unless three-fifths of the whole House and three-fifths of the whole Senate vote to incur a deficit. The resolution waives the balanced budget requirement for any fiscal year in which a declaration of war is in effect or the United States is engaged in an "imminent and serious threat to national security." A joint resolution indicating this situation must be adopted by a majority of the total membership of both the House and the Senate, and must be signed by the President.

The bill stipulates that the federal public debt will be limited to its level on the first day of the second fiscal year beginning after ratification of the balanced budget amendment. The limit may only be increased by a three-fifths roll call vote in each chamber. Tax increases must also be approved by a three-fifths majority of the membership of each house.

Finally, the bill mandates that all associated votes must be on the record roll call votes, and that the balanced budget requirement will take effect in FY 2002 or the second fiscal year after it is ratified, whichever is later.

### Line-Item Veto

The Fiscal Responsibility Act gives the President a permanent legislative line-item veto. Under this procedure, the President could strike any appropriation or targeted tax provision (a provision that provides special treatment to a particular taxpayer or limited class of taxpayers) in any bill.

The President is required to submit his rescission proposal within twenty calendar days (not including weekends or holidays) after Congress finally passes a bill or resolution and must submit a separate rescission proposal for each piece of legislation. The President's proposed rescissions are to take effect unless Congress disapproves them in an up-or-down vote within twenty days after receipt of the proposal. If the President vetoes the disapproval bill, Congress would have to override it by a two-thirds vote.

The bill also sets forth the procedures for Senate consideration of a proposed rescission, including limiting debate time on a disapproval bill to ten hours.

Finally, the Fiscal Responsibility Act limits a disapproval bill to only those matters relating to the proposed rescissions transmitted by the President and stipulates that a disapproval bill is unamendable. These provisions, however, are made in accordance with House rules and may be waived by the House Rules Committee at any point.

### Myths versus Facts

**Myth:** Republicans want to incorporate their economic policies into the Constitution.

**Fact:** The Founding Fathers explicitly addressed economic issues throughout the Constitution. Tax policy, monetary policy, trade, regulation, and private property rights are some of the many economic issues dealt with in the Constitution. At issue is whether a balanced budget amendment is needed to correct a systematic flaw in the political system. With the national debt over $3.4 trillion, and with the Congressional Budget Office projecting deficits of nearly $400 billion in less than a decade, the answer is yes.

**Myth:** The balanced budget amendment is a superficial gimmick, another means to avoid making real choices about how to balance the budget.

**Fact:** To the contrary, a balanced budget amendment would force lawmakers to make the hard choices. Unable to increase spending today at the expense of future generations, lawmakers would have little choice but to make definitive fiscal priorities and to make long-overdue reforms in federal programs.

**Myth:** A balanced budget amendment would necessitate massive tax increases and cuts in Social Security benefits.

**Fact:** The Republican balanced budget amendment contains a tax limitation provision that would not allow Congress to resort to massive tax increases to balance the budget. Moreover, Social Security need not be cut one cent to balance the budget. The first step toward fiscal responsibility would be to question the hundreds of billions of dollars in new federal spending proposed by Bill Clinton.

**Myth:** A line-item veto would give the President too much power.

**Fact:** A line-item veto would restore the balance between the President and the Congress. In the mid-1970s, the Congress upset the existing balance when it changed the budget process and consciously undermined the President's ability to constrain the growth of federal spending. Ever since these process reforms, the Congress has been able to simply ignore the President's budget rescission requests. The line-item veto proposed by Republicans forces the Congress to debate and vote upon the President's rescission proposals. Balance would be restored.

**Myth:** A line-item veto would not solve the deficit problem.

**Fact:** By itself, a line-item veto would not solve the deficit problem overnight. But it would move us toward fiscal responsibility. It would enable the President to slash the pork residing in the federal budget. It would also allow the Congress to disagree with the President. The Congress could restore spending cuts by the President, if it thought the President's package of rescissions was inappropriate.

## *Further Reading*

*Arguments For and Against:* "We Need to Amend Our Ways—Not the Constitution," by Sen. Nancy Landon Kassebaum, *The Washington Post*, March 1, 1994, p. A20; "Balanced Budget Bogyman," by David S. Broder, *The Washington Post*, February 27, 1994, p. C7; "Stop and Consider the Consequences of Balanced Budget," by Norman J. Ornstein, *Roll Call*, February 21, 1994, p. 16; "An Unbalanced Constitution," by Lloyd N. Cutler, *The Washington Post*, February 16, 1994, p. A19; "Balanced Budget Bill Is Opposed," *The Washington Post*, February 13, 1994, p. A5; "Why America Needs a Balanced Budget Amendment," The Heritage Foundation *Backgrounder*#204, October 15, 1993; "Line Item Veto and Rescission Authority," *Congressional Digest*, February 1993; and "Balanced Budget Constitutional Amendment—Pro and Con," *Congressional Digest*, November 1989.

# *Stop Violent Criminals*

ISN'T AN ESSENTIAL part of the American Dream the freedom from fear? The American Dream cannot survive without safety and security for individual Americans—for all of you. When our children are afraid to go to school, when husbands and wives are afraid to walk to the grocery store, and when society as a whole is being threatened, government must meet its responsibility to protect our streets, our schools, and our neighborhoods.

Our *Contract with America* calls for tough punishment for those who prey on society. For too long, Washington has refused to get tough—and even when they sound tough, there are always loopholes that favor the criminal, not the victims. Our *Contract* will make the death penalty real—no more endless appeals.

We will cut the "pork" in the recently passed crime bill in order to build real prisons, and we will require criminals to serve their sentences, not have them back on the street to terrorize again and again. And to make criminals more accountable, we will force them to pay full restitution to their victims or the victims' families.

And to those who commit felonies with guns, let us be particularly clear: We will require ten years in jail, minimum, no exceptions.

We call this bill the Taking Back Our Streets Act, and it will be voted on in the first hundred days of a Republican House of Representatives. It's time for all of us to feel safe and secure once again.

## *The Taking Back Our Streets Act*

There was a time when criminals knew that if they committed a violent crime, they would be punished severely. But during the 1960s and 1970s, liberals—both members of Congress and members of the bench and bar—declared war on swift and certain punishment.

The Taking Back Our Streets Act embodies the Republican approach to fighting crime: making punishments severe enough to deter criminals from committing crimes, making sure that the criminal justice system is fair and impartial for all, and making sure that local law enforcement officials (who are on the streets every day) and not Washington bureaucrats direct the distribution of federal law enforcement funds.

The bill sets mandatory sentences for crimes involving the use of firearms, authorizes $10.5 billion for state prison construction grants, establishes truth-in-sentencing guidelines, reforms the habeas corpus appeals process, allows police officers who in good faith seized incriminating evidence in violation of the "exclusionary rule" to use the evidence in court, requires that convicted criminals make restitution to their victims, and authorizes $10 billion for local law enforcement spending. Finally, in addressing one of the most pressing problems in our country today, the bill streamlines the current alien deportation system, while still allowing convicted aliens the right to judicial review and appeal.

This legislation strikes at the heart of our violent crime problem by deterring criminals from committing crimes in the first place, and making sure that if they do commit a crime, they serve the sentence they are given and are not able to abuse the appeals process. This bill fixes a number of problems created by the recently enacted omnibus crime bill, as well as serious problems left unaddressed by that legislation. Critics maintain that the measure concentrates too much on punishment and not enough on prevention; the way to stop crime, they argue, is not to keep filling our jails, but to keep at-risk youth from going there in the first place.

## Background

Statistics paint a grim picture, illustrating clearly that the United States has failed to get a handle on its growing crime problem. One expert has estimated that a twenty-year-old black male has a greater chance of being murdered on the streets than a soldier in World War II stood of dying in combat. According to the FBI, the rate of violent crime in the United States is worse than in any other Western country, with a murder occurring every twenty-one minutes, a rape every five minutes, a robbery every forty-six seconds and an aggravated assault every twenty-nine seconds. Violent crime or property crime victimizes one in four U.S. households. Every year, nearly five million people are victims of violent crime such as murder, rape, robbery, or assault, and 19 million Americans are victims of property crimes such as arson or burglary. Juvenile crime has increased by 60 percent between 1981 and 1990 (compared with an increase of 5 percent among adults), and the number of inmates convicted of drug offenses rose 14 percent from 1983 to 1989. On all fronts, the problem has reached epidemic proportions.

This crime crisis is particularly severe among minorities and the poor. The U.S. homicide rate for black males between the ages of fifteen and twenty-four is 283 times that of male homicide rates in seventeen other nations. And homicide is now the leading cause of death for blacks aged fifteen to thirty-four. Poor households are victimized more often than upper-income households. In 1992, households with incomes of less than $7,500 experienced crime at a rate of 136.7 per 1,000 compared with the rate of 83.3 per 1,000 for households with incomes between $30,000 and $49,000.

While the problem is severe, statistics illustrate that a small percentage of criminals commit the vast majority of violent crimes. A small percentage of career criminals commit a majority of violent crimes. A 1991 study done by the Bureau of Alcohol, Tobacco, and Firearms indicated that 471 armed criminals had a total of 3,088 felony convictions—an average of 6.55 felonies each. To make matters worse, many of these criminals either are never caught, or, if found guilty, do not serve their entire prison sentence. Every year, over 60,000 criminals convicted of a violent crime never go to prison—for every hundred crimes reported only three criminals go to prison. The Bureau of Justice Statistics has found that only 45.4 percent of court-ordered confinement is served on average, and 51 percent of violent offenders sent to prison are released in two years or less. These numbers are even more telling in light of the fact that at least 30 percent of the murders in this country are committed by people on probation, parole, or bail. Faced with prison overcrowding, seventeen states have begun emergency release programs. Overall, the risk of punishment has declined in the past forty years while the annual number of serious crimes committed has skyrocketed.

All this has led to public calls for truth-in-sentencing laws (requiring criminals to serve a significant percentage of their sentences without a chance of parole) and "three strikes, you're out" laws (requiring life in prison for repeat offenders convicted of their third violent felony). Opponents of strict sentencing laws like these argue that locking people up does not address the problem of why crimes are committed in the first place. Evidence suggests, however, that there is a strong correlation between increased incarceration and decreased crime rates: from 1990 to 1991, states with the greatest increases in criminal incarceration rates experienced, on average, a 12.7 percent decrease in crime, while the ten states with the weakest incarceration rates experienced an average 6.9 percent increase in crime.

## Recent Legislation

Recently, President Clinton signed the Omnibus Crime Control Act of 1994 after nearly one year of congressional hearings, mark-ups, floor votes, conference wrangling, a delayed recess, and weekend votes. Many members spoke out against the legislation, arguing that it did little to address the fundamental crime problem in our country. Relying on expensive "Great

Society-esque" programs, the bill attempted to do what all other big government social programs have failed to do: make individuals responsible for their actions and instill a sense of right and wrong in those with a propensity to commit a crime. Criticism focused not only on what the bill contained, but on what it lacked. Republicans argued that it should have included reform of the habeas corpus process (the process by which inmates challenge the constitutionality of their sentences), a good faith exemption for the exclusionary rule, tough language against sexual predators, more money for state prison construction, and stronger requirements that states enact truth-in-sentencing laws to be eligible for grant assistance.

After a crazy weekend session at the end of August, the conference agreement was finally approved by the House 235–195. When all was said and done, the compromise authorized a total of $30 billion over six years, including $5.4 billion for prevention programs, $7.9 billion for new prison construction and $8.8 billion for new police officers. It also included the so-called "three strikes, you're out" provision, applied the death penalty to over fifty new crimes, increased penalties for repeat federal sex offenders, and banned at least 150 semiautomatic weapons. The final version did not include the controversial Racial Justice Act (which allows defendants to introduce in their defense statistical evidence that blacks receive death sentences more often than whites) or any reform of the habeas corpus process.

In addition to passing the first omnibus crime bill in four years, the 103rd Congress also passed the Brady

Bill, which established a five-day waiting period for the purchase of a handgun. The House approved that measure on November 10, 1993, by a vote of 238–189. President Clinton signed it into law on November 30, 1993. Other smaller crime-related bills passed during this Congress include the National Child Protection Act of 1993, which established criminal background checks for child care providers, and the International Parental Kidnapping Crime Act, which made it a federal crime for a parent to kidnap a child under the age of sixteen years from his custodial parent and remove him from the United States.

Here's what *Contract with America* proposes:

### General Habeas Corpus Reform

The bill makes a number of revisions to federal and state habeas corpus processes (the process by which prisoners who have exhausted all direct appeals challenge the constitutionality of their sentences). Specifically, it places a one-year limitation on the filing of general federal habeas corpus appeals after all state remedies have been exhausted. State capital cases must be filed in a federal court within six months, and state capital prisoners who file a second or successive federal habeas appeal must receive a certificate of probable cause stating that their case has merit. Noncapital federal prisoners must file within two years. The bill also forces federal courts to consider federal habeas petitions within a certain time frame.

In addition to placing a time limit on when federal appeals may be made, the Taking Back Our Streets

Act limits prisoners to one appeal unless the defendant can show by "clear and convincing evidence, that but for Constitutional error, no reasonable fact finder would have found [him or her] guilty of the underlying offense or eligible for the death penalty."

Under current law, there are virtually no limits or restrictions on when prisoners can file habeas corpus appeals. For example, under current law, defendants can appeal any time there is a change in the law or a new Supreme Court ruling. Delays of up to fourteen years are not uncommon, making abuse of the habeas corpus system the most significant factor in states' inability to implement credible death penalties. Current law favors the convicted criminal. For example, the recently enacted crime legislation included a requirement that at least *two* lawyers be appointed to represent the defendant at every stage of the process.

Latin for "you should have the body," habeas corpus is used to determine whether a person is lawfully imprisoned. Originally designed as a remedy for imprisonment without trial, it is now a tool of federal and state defendants who have been convicted and exhausted all direct appeals (prisoners currently have three successive procedures to challenge a conviction or sentence: appeal, state habeas corpus, and federal habeas corpus). Critics of the current habeas corpus process argue that (1) most petitions are totally lacking in merit, (2) thousands upon thousands of frivolous petitions clog the federal district court dockets each year, and (3) it allows prisoners on death row to almost indefinitely delay their punishment.

***Authorization of Funds for States to Prosecute Capital Cases:*** Congress already provides funds for death penalty resource centers to litigate federal habeas corpus petitions for death row inmates. The Taking Back Our Streets Act authorizes equal funding for states to prosecute these cases.

***Reform of Death Penalty Procedures:*** The bill mandates that juries be instructed to recommend a death sentence if aggravating factors (circumstances of the crime that increase the level of guilt) outweigh mitigating factors (circumstances that reduce the degree of moral culpability). Juries must also be instructed to avoid any "influence of sympathy, sentiment, passion, prejudice or other arbitrary factors" in their decisions.

Under the recent Omnibus Crime Control Act, the Justice Department is required to notify the court and the defendant that it intends to seek the death penalty, and it must indicate the aggravating factors it intends to prove as the basis for imposition of a capital sentence. The law specifically states that a jury is never required to impose a death sentence (even if it finds that aggravating factors outweigh mitigating factors), and that death penalties can never be imposed on individuals who are mentally retarded, incompetent, or under eighteen years of age at the time of their crime. Critics of current law argue that it (1) establishes an elaborate system of aggravating and mitigating factors, but then allows juries to ignore the evidence and make an arbitrary sentencing recommendation; (2) gives too much discretion to a judge and jury; (3) weakens current law; and (4) greatly complicates the use of any new federal death penalty.

## Mandatory Minimum Sentencing for Drug Crimes

The Comprehensive Crime Control Act of 1984 created the U.S. Sentencing Commission to develop and monitor sentencing guidelines to be used by federal judges when sentencing criminal defendants. Despite the commission's suggestions that mandatory minimum sentences tend to warp the guidelines system, Congress has enacted about one hundred mandatory minimum sentences for a variety of federal crimes. Many federal judges have complained that these restrictions are foolish, wasteful, and cruel (sometimes requiring them to impose a sentence without regard to the nature of the offense or the character and background of the offender), and that they have no deterrent effect on crime.

Supporters of mandatory sentences counter that they complement the sentencing guidelines, prevent disparity in sentencing, and ensure certainty of punishment. Mandatory minimums send a strong and unmistakable message to criminals that they will serve a set minimum sentence if they commit certain violent crimes. Mandatory minimums are also used by prosecutors to extract confessions from low-level offenders in exchange for reduced sentences. The information is then used to build cases against criminal crime bosses. Although judges object to mandatory minimums because they take away their sentencing discretion, prosecutors see them as important law enforcement tools.

The Taking Back Our Streets Act establishes a mandatory minimum sentence of ten years for state or federal drug or violent crimes that involve possession of a gun. Penalties increase to twenty years for a second conviction and life in prison for a third. For those who discharge a firearm with intent to injure another person, the first offense is punishable by a minimum of twenty years in prison, second offenses are punishable by a minimum of thirty years, and third violations get life in prison.

Finally, possession or use of a machine gun or other destructive device during the commission of these crimes is punishable for no less than thirty years. Second-time offenses are punishable by life in prison.

## *Mandatory Victim Restitution*

For the last forty years, victims of violent crime have been the forgotten casualties in our surrender to violent crime. The Taking Back Our Streets Act mandates that criminals pay full restitution to their victims for damages caused as a result of the crime. (Current law allows the court to order that such restitution be made but it does not require it.) In addition, the bill allows (but does not require) the court to order restitution of *any* person who, as shown by a preponderance of the evidence, was harmed physically, emotionally or financially by the unlawful conduct of the defendant.

***Court Responsibility:*** Under the bill, restitution is to reimburse the victim for necessary child care, transportation, and other expenses incurred while participating in the investigation or court proceedings. The court is to determine the amount of restitution based on the victim's situation and not on the economic resources of the offender or the fact that the victim is entitled to insurance or other compensation. The court is also to set the payment schedule (for example, a single lump-sum payment or a partial payment at specified intervals) and method of payment (for example, cash, return of property, or replacement of property).

***Limitations on Restitution Awards:*** Court-ordered compensation is not to affect the victim's eligibility to receive insurance awards or other compensation until such time that the court-ordered compensation fully compensates the victim for his losses. In addition, the bill stipulates that if the claimant seeks additional awards in a civil case, any new award is to be reduced by the amount of the criminal court restitution order (bill supporters argue that claimants may seek additional awards but should not be able to receive a second full compensation).

***Defendant Compliance:*** Compliance with the schedule of payment and other terms of the restitution order is a condition for probation, parole or any other form of release. If the defendant fails to comply with the restitution order, the court may revoke probation or parole, modify the conditions of probation or parole, hold the defendant in contempt of court, enter a restraining order or injunction against the defendant, order the sale of the defendant's property, or take any other action necessary to insure compliance with the restitution order. The victim or offender may at any time petition the court to modify a restitution order if the offender's economic circumstances change.

## *Law Enforcement Block Grants*

The crime bill passed by Congress in August 1994 contains so many compartmentalized programs for prevention and so many strings to grants to hire police officers, many cities and states have given up on these funds. The Taking Back Our Streets Act authorizes a total of $10 billion over five years ($2 billion in each of FY 1996–2000) for local governments to fund law enforcement programs. These block grants replace the police, prevention, and drug courts titles of the recently enacted crime bill. Under the bill, money may be used to (1) hire, train, or employ law enforcement officers; (2) pay overtime to police officers; (3) purchase equipment and technology directly related to basic law enforcement purposes; (4) enhance school security measures (for example, police patrols around school grounds, metal detectors, fences, closed circuit cameras, gun hotlines, et cetera); (5) establish citizen neighborhood watch programs; and/or (6) fund programs that advance moral standards and the values of citizenship and involve local law enforcement officials.

To qualify for these grants, a unit of local government must show that it will (1) establish a trust fund in which block grant money is to be deposited; (2) use the money within two years; (3) spend the money in accordance with the guidelines in this section; (4) use approved accounting, audit, and fiscal procedures; (5) make any requested records available to the Bureau of Justice Assistance and the comptroller of the United States for review; and (6) submit the required progress reports. Each state that applies is to automatically receive 0.25 percent of the funds as well as additional funds based on its number of reported violent crimes in 1993 compared to the rest of the country. States are to distribute the funds among local units of government based on their population and the number of reported violent crimes in 1993 compared with the rest of the local governmental units in the state.

If a unit of local government does not spend all of its grant money within two years of receipt, it must repay the unused portion to the Bureau of Justice Assistance within three months. The bill also stipulates that (1) this grant money is intended to supplement, not supplant, state funds; (2) grantees may not use more than 2.5 percent of their grant for administrative costs; and (3) grantees must hold one public hearing on the proposed use of their grant. The bill also sets out procedures to be used if a local government violates any portion of this title.

As noted above, the Taking Back Our Streets Act repeals sections of the recently enacted crime control act that provide specific funds for drug courts, recreational programs, community justice programs, and other social prevention spending. Bill sponsors argue that providing money directly to local law enforcers and letting them decide how to spend the funds (as the Taking Back Our Streets Act does) is preferable to the current law approach of authorizing specific amounts of money for programs approved by Washington bureaucrats.

## *Grants for Prison Construction Based on Truth in Sentencing*

In America today violent criminals serve only about one-third of their prison sentence. The Taking Back Our Streets Act authorizes $10.5 billion over six years ($232 million in FY 1995, $997.5 million in FY 1996, $1.3 billion in FY 1997, $2.5 billion in FY 1998, $2.7 billion in FY 1999 and $2.8 billion in FY 2000) for the Attorney General to make grants to states so they can build, expand, and operate prisons for serious violent felons. This title replaces the prison section in the recently enacted crime bill. The bill also authorizes the Attorney General to make grants for states to move nonviolent offenders and criminal aliens to other correctional facilities (including old military bases) to make room for violent criminals at existing prisons. Grants are to be awarded based on two formulas: a percentage that applies to all states (.40 percent) and a percentage based on population.

Fifty percent of the funds authorized under this section are designated as "general grants." To receive these funds, states must show that since 1993 (1) an increased percentage of convicted violent offenders have been sentenced to prison, (2) the state has increased the average prison time actually served in prison, and

(3) the state has increased the percentage of sentences to be actually served. The other 50 percent is reserved for truth-in-sentencing incentive grants. To be eligible for these funds, states must show that they require serious violent felons to serve at least 85 percent of the sentence imposed, and require sentencing or releasing authorities to allow the defendant's victim (or the victim's family) to testify on the issue of sentencing and any post-conviction release.

The bill includes an exception for prisoners over the age of seventy years after a public hearing in which representatives of the public and the prisoner's victims have an opportunity to testify on the issue of release. It also stipulates that (1) grant money is to supplement, not supplant, state funds; (2) no more than 3 percent of the grant is to be used by states for administrative costs; (3) the federal share of a grant is not to exceed 75 percent of the total cost of a state proposal; and (4) any funds not spent in one year will carry over and remain available until spent.

## Reform of the Exclusionary Rule

The Supreme Court enforces the Constitution's Fourth Amendment (which protects Americans against unreasonable searches and seizures) through the so-called exclusionary rule. The rule holds that any evidence discovered as a result of improper police action cannot be introduced in a federal or state criminal trial—i.e., "the criminal is to go free because the constable has blundered." Critics of the rule's rigidity argue that it suppresses evidence of unquestionable reliability and leads to the acquittal of many who are obviously guilty. In 1984, the Supreme Court modified the exclusionary rule to permit the introduction of evidence that was obtained in good faith reliance on a search warrant that was later found to be invalid. However, many have called for a "good faith exemption" in cases where the police officer, acting in good faith, conducted a search or seizure without a warrant.

The Taking Back Our Streets Act amends current law to allow introduction of evidence obtained during a search or seizure that was conducted with the objectively reasonable belief that it was in accordance with the Fourth Amendment, regardless of whether a search warrant had been granted.

## Prisoner Lawsuits

States are forced to spend millions of dollars defending prisoner lawsuits to improve prison conditions—many of which are frivolous. Critics of the proposal argue that it will restrict prisoners' rights to seek legitimate redress of grievances.

The Taking Back Our Streets Act directs federal courts to dismiss any frivolous or malicious suit brought by an adult convicted of a crime and confined in any jail, prison, or other correctional facility. The bill also requires that prisoners filing a suit include a statement of all assets in their possession so the court can require a full or partial payment of filing fees based on the prisoner's ability to pay.

## Deportation of Criminal Aliens

States today spend hundreds of millions of dollars holding illegal aliens convicted of violent crimes. This title of the bill provides for the prompt deportation of any alien without a green card who has been convicted of an aggravated felony and who is deportable. It addresses the current problem of releasing these felons into the general population prior to finalization of deportation proceedings, since few of those released ever show up for their deportation hearings.

**Definition of an Aggravated Felony:** For purposes of alien felon deportation, the bill expands the definition of an aggravated felony to include any state or federal offense involving (1) firearms violations; (2) failure to appear in court for a felony carrying a sentence of two or more years; (3) demanding or receiving ransom money; (4) a RICO violation; (5) owning, controlling, managing, or supervising a prostitution business; (6) treason; (7) tax evasion exceeding $200,000; and (8) certain immigration-related offenses including alien smuggling and sale of fraudulent documents. Supporters argue that these crimes are serious enough to put a convicted alien on the fast track for deportation.

The current law definition of an aggravated felony includes murder, drug trafficking, trafficking in firearms or explosives, money laundering, terrorism, and any crime of violence carrying a prison sentence of at least five years.

***Criminal Alien Deportation Proceedings:*** The bill allows the Attorney General to issue a final order of deportation against any alien determined to be deportable for conviction of an aggravated felony (without requiring a deportation hearing). An alien is defined as anyone who (1) was not lawfully admitted for permanent residence in the United States at the time that proceedings for the commission of an aggravated crime began or (2) had permanent resident status on a conditional basis at the time that proceedings for the commission of an aggravated crime began. An alien against whom a deportation order is issued may appeal for judicial review in federal court; however, the court action is limited to challenging only the defendant's identification (whether the person is who the Immigration and Naturalization Service [INS] says he is and whether he committed the aggravated felony).

***Judicial Deportations:*** When an alien whose conviction causes him to be deemed deportable is sentenced, a federal court may issue a judicial order of deportation if the U.S. attorney requested one prior to sentencing and the INS commissioner is in agreement. A judicial order of deportation or a denial of such order may be appealed by either party to the circuit court of appeals. A court action, however, is limited to challenging only the defendant's identification (whether the person is who the Immigration and Naturalization Service [INS] says he is and whether he committed the aggravated felony). If a judicial order is denied, the Attorney General may still pursue a deportation order through administrative channels.

***Defenses Based on Permanent Residence:*** Under current law, when an alien is in deportation proceedings, he can use certain defenses to get out. One such defense is showing that he has been a permanent resident of the United States for the past seven years. The Taking Back Our Streets Act does not change the underlying defense, but changes the time frame in which INS can begin deportation proceedings against an alien convicted of an aggravated offense. Under current law, deportation proceedings are to begin after the alien has served five years. The Taking Back Our Streets Act allows INS to begin deportation proceedings when an alien is sentenced to a term of at least five years. This standard is more relevant for judging the seriousness of a crime, since dangerous criminals may be released prematurely due to prison overcrowding or for other reasons not related to the seriousness of the crime.

***Defenses Based on Withholding of Deportation:*** Aliens may also reverse deportation proceedings by showing that they will suffer physical harm if returned to their native country. As defined by international law, "withholding of deportation" is a higher standard of protection than asylum: If an alien can prove such a situation exists, he must be retained in the United States unless he poses a danger to the public. The Taking Back Our Streets Act clarifies current law to stipulate that aggravated felons pose a serious danger to the public and are not allowed to request or be granted this protection.

***Enhanced Penalties for Failing to Deport or Reentering:*** Under current law, aliens who are deportable for criminal offenses, for document fraud, or because they are a security risk to the United States face up to ten years in prison for failure to depart. Bill sponsors argue that there are no penalties for aliens who are deportable for other reasons but refuse to leave. The Taking Back Our Streets Act retains the current law penalty and establishes a penalty of up to four years in prison for all other deportable aliens who refuse to leave. The bill also establishes civil penalties for those who refuse to leave.

Under current law, an alien who is convicted of a felony (other than an aggravated offense), is deported, and then reenters the country is subject to five years in prison and a criminal fine. The Taking Back Our Streets Act extends such penalties to aliens convicted of three or more misdemeanors and increases the maximum sentence to ten years. Deported aggravated felons who reenter the United States are currently subject to criminal fines and up to fifteen years in prison. The Taking Back Our Streets Act increases the maximum prison sentence to twenty years.

Finally, under the bill, a deported alien who reenters the United States cannot challenge his original deportation unless he can show that (1) all available administrative remedies were exhausted, (2) an opportunity for judicial review was denied, and (3) the deportation order was fundamentally unfair.

***Criminal Alien Tracking Center:*** The bill directs the INS commissioner and the director of the FBI, with the heads of other agencies, to operate a criminal tracking center. The measure authorizes $14 million over four years ($5 million in FY 1994 and $2 million in each of FY 1995–98) for the center, which is to assist federal, state, and local law enforcement agencies identify and locate aliens who may be subject to deportation due to conviction of an aggravated felony.

## Myths versus Facts

**Myth:** Democrats and Republicans spent months putting together the most comprehensive crime bill possible and Clinton signed it into law. Now Republicans just can't accept the fact that they lost on the crime bill. They won't admit that Democrats can also be tough on crime and Republicans are trying to change what happened to regain ownership of the crime issue.

**Fact:** Democrats crafted a crime bill loaded down with worn-out, ineffective social welfare programs and pork-barrel spending. They then used their majority status to waive congressional rules and disallow Republican opportunities to improve the bill. The Democrats squandered this year's opportunity to enact sweeping change in our dysfunctional criminal justice system. They passed a $30 billion bill that will fight crime with weakened justice provisions, federally dictated midnight basketball, arts and crafts. We believe this *Con-*

*tract* lays the groundwork for a genuine no-nonsense assault on crime that will reap results.

**Myth:** The *Contract* seeks to ease the restrictions dictating how state and local governments can qualify for and spend their money for prevention and police. If Republicans *really* intended for local communities to have true control over their crime-fighting dollars, they would free restrictions on qualifying for and spending *prison funds* as well. The truth-in-sentencing provisions proposed in the *Contract* are too restrictive and should allow states to provide alternatives for incarceration to free up space for low-level offenders who don't need to be in prison.

**Fact:** Today, *two-thirds* of state prison inmates have been convicted of a violent crime and almost *95 percent* of state prison inmates are either convicted violent offenders or convicted repeat offenders. Which criminals do Democrats recommend be released to free up much-needed prison space? Fewer than one in ten serious crimes result in imprisonment, and 30 percent of all violent crime today is committed by individuals while they are out on pretrial release, bail, or parole. Crime rates soar as a result of the system's inability to incapacitate violent repeat offenders and keep them beyond a fraction of their sentence. We have national consensus on the urgent need to lock up violent criminals and ensure the safety of our communities. There is *not* consensus, however, on the effectiveness of one-size-fits-all federal prevention programs or how to federally place a police force—these are decisions that are best made at the local level, closest to the problem.

**Myth:** The *Contract* is disingenuous about providing local control of crime funds. What they really want is a bill that focuses only on police and prisons with no prevention funding.

**Fact:** While the *Contract* asserts the need for swift and certain punishment for criminals, it does not assault the merits of prevention programs. The proposed legislation will leave the discretion with local officials who are closest to the problem. Only they can determine their specific needs and the solutions to address the crime in their communities. The proposed legislation asks only that prevention programs involve law enforcement organizations and truly address the crime problems of that community. This is a clear contrast to the crime bill that contains billions in one-size-fits-all social welfare programs that have nothing to do with crime and pork-barrel handouts to political cronies.

**Myth:** The proposed legislation that requires mandatory minimum sentences for the use of a gun during the commission of a state or federal felony is intrusive on states rights and will overwhelm the federal courts with thousands of new cases. It essentially federalizes all gun crimes.

**Fact:** The proposed legislation provides prosecutors with the *option* of taking a state gun crime to the federal courts—it doesn't require it. This provision gives overburdened state and local law enforcement access to tougher federal tools including mandatory sentences and a functioning prison system that guarantees truth-in-sentencing. America's worst violent criminals can be taken into the federal system, where they will be more likely to serve a full prison sentence and will be less likely to be released early, back onto the streets to commit more deadly crimes.

**Myth:** The *Contract* seeks to diminish guaranteed constitutional rights of prison inmates. History has shown serious abuses taking place in our prison systems and inmates have a right to be heard.

**Fact:** The *Contract* does not seek to diminish the rights of prison inmates. However, there is an alarming trend taking place in our court systems—prisoner grievances have grown to consume over a quarter of the civil docket in some states. Many prisoners use the system to harass prison officials or to delay sentencing—over 90 percent of these cases are eventually deemed groundless by the courts. Prisoners have asserted that a lack of Frisbees, art supplies, and chunky peanut butter (as opposed to creamy peanut butter) constitutes cruel and unusual punishment. These cases cost millions of dollars in resources and could be resolved through administrative remedy without resorting to federal court. This legislation seeks to reduce *frivolous* prisoner litigation and encourage states to adopt grievance dispute measures that adequately substitute for judicial hearings.

**Myth:** The *Contract* seeks to diminish defendants' guaranteed constitutional rights against unreasonable searches and seizures by the government. The proposed legislation tampers with the exclusionary rule, which prohibits use of illegally obtained evidence in a criminal trial if that evidence was obtained illegally or improperly. The proposed legislation will allow police officers to abuse search and seizure laws and unfairly collect evidence.

**Fact:** In recent years, the Supreme Court has identified a number of situations where it has declined to apply the exclusionary rule. The court has established a "good faith" exception to the exclusionary rule that permits use of improperly obtained evidence in cases where police *thought* they were acting legally. The proposed legislation seeks to codify and extend the good faith exception to enhance the truth-seeking function of the criminal trial. Too many guilty go free because of simple technical errors committed by officers who believed they were conducting proper investigations. A decade ago, an estimated 45,000 to 55,000 felony and serious misdemeanor cases were dropped because of problems created by the exclusionary rule. The proposed legislation contains safeguards that prohibit police abuse of constitutional rights while at the same time closes the legal loopholes that let criminals go free.

## Further Reading

***Critique of the Recent Crime Bill:*** "The Crime Bill: Few Cops, Many Social Workers," The Heritage Foundation *Issue Bulletin*, August 2, 1994; "What's Wrong with the Brooks and Biden Crime Bills," The Heritage Foundation *Issue Bulletin*, November 8, 1993; "On the Firing Line: Clinton's Crime Bill," The Heritage Foundation's *Lecture 476*, September 24, 1993; and "How States Can Fight Violent Crime: Two Dozen Steps to a Safer America," The Heritage Foundation *State Backgrounder*, June 7, 1993.

***Capital Punishment:*** "47 New Death Penalties. Big Deal," by Robert M. Morgenthau, *The New York Times*, November 10, 1993, p. A27.

***Mandatory Minimums:*** "Congressional Overkill," by Judiciary Civil and Constitutional Rights Subcommittee Chairman Edwards, *The Washington Post*, March 8, 1994, p. A19; "Justice Kennedy Assails Mandatory Sentences," *The Washington Post*, March 10, 1994, p. A15; "What Prosecutors Know: Mandatory Minimums Work," by Jay Apperson, *The Washington Post*, February 27, 1994, p. C1; "Mandatory Minimums and the Betrayal of Sentencing Reform" by Henry Scott Wallace and "Mandatory Minimum Sentences: A Federal Prosecutor's Viewpoint" by Michael M. Baylson,

*Federal Bar News & Journal,* March/April 1993, Vol. 40; and "Crime, Punishment and Politics," *The Washington Post,* October 6, 1993, p. A23.

**Three Strikes:** "We've Got Three Strikes—It's Working," by John Carlson, *The Washington Post,* March 6, 1994, p. C7; "What Pols Won't Say: 'Three Strikes—and We're Out of Money,'" *The Washington Post,* February 27, 1994, p. C1; "Critics Say Three Strikes Proposal Would Do Little to Reduce Crime," *The Washington Post,* February 22, 1994, p. A4; "When to Call Three Strikes," *The Washington Post,* February 1, 1994, p. A20; and "Violent Crime Strikes a Chord Coast to Coast," *The Washington Post,* January 24, 1994, p. A1.

**Truth in Sentencing:** "Truth in Sentencing: Why States Should Make Violent Criminals Do Their Time," The Heritage Foundation *State Backgrounder,* December 30, 1993.

# Welfare Reform

ISN'T IT TIME for the government to encourage work rather than rewarding dependency? The Great Society has had the unintended consequence of snaring millions of Americans into the welfare trap. Government programs designed to give a helping hand to the neediest of Americans have instead bred illegitimacy, crime, illiteracy, and more poverty. Our *Contract with America* will change this destructive social behavior by requiring welfare recipients to take personal responsibility for the decisions they make. Our *Contract* will achieve what some thirty years of massive welfare spending has not been able to accomplish: reduce illegitimacy, require work, and save taxpayers money.

To reverse skyrocketing out-of-wedlock births that are ripping apart our nation's social fabric, we provide no welfare to teenage parents and we require that paternity and responsibility be established in all illegitimate births where welfare is sought.

To ensure that welfare offers a helping hand rather than a handout, we require that welfare beneficiaries work so they can develop the pride and self-sufficiency that comes from holding a productive job. We are pledging truly to "end welfare as we know it."

America can still be the land of opportunity for all Americans. But to succeed, we must make a break from the failed welfare policies of the past. Within the first one hundred days of a Republican Congress we will do just that by voting on the Personal Responsibility Act.

## *The Personal Responsibility Act*

The Personal Responsibility Act overhauls the American welfare system to reduce government dependency, attack illegitimacy, require welfare recipients to work, and cut welfare spending. The legislation's main thrust is to give states greater control over the benefits programs, work programs, and Aid to Families with Dependent Children (AFDC) payments and requirements.

Under the bill, the structure for AFDC payments will drastically change. Mothers under the age of eighteen may no longer receive AFDC payments for children born out of wedlock and mothers who are ages eighteen, nineteen, and twenty can be prohibited by the states from receiving AFDC payments and housing benefits. Mothers must also identify the fathers as a condition for receiving AFDC payments, except in cases of rape and incest. Also, in order to reduce the amount of time families are on welfare, states must begin moving welfare recipients into work programs if they have received welfare for two years. States are given the option to drop families from receiving AFDC benefits after they have received welfare for two years if at least one year has been spent in a work program. To further limit the length of time on AFDC, states must drop families from the program after they have received a total of five years of AFDC benefits.

The Personal Responsibility Act allows states to design their own work programs and determine who will be required to participate. Welfare recipients must work an average of thirty-five hours a week or enroll in work training programs. By the year 2001, 1.5 million AFDC recipients will be required to work.

The bill caps the spending growth of several major welfare programs (AFDC, Supplemental Security Income [SSI] and public housing) and consolidates ten nutrition programs, including food stamps, WIC, and the school lunch program, into one discretionary block grant to states.

Finally, the Personal Responsibility Act grants greater flexibility to states allowing them to design their own work programs and determine who participates in them and can choose to opt out of the current AFDC program by converting their share of AFDC payments into fixed annual block grants.

### Background

In the mid-1960s President Lyndon Johnson launched a war on poverty with the hope of creating a Great Society. The federal government was mobilized to fight poverty by creating a slew of new federal programs and expanding existing ones, such as AFDC. More than twenty-five years later, Johnson's War on Poverty has been an unqualified failure. Despite spending trillions of dollars, it has had the unintended consequence of making welfare more attractive than work to many families, and once welfare recipients become dependent on public assistance, they are caught in the now-familiar welfare trap.

Established in 1935 under the Social Security Act, AFDC was created to help widows care for their children. It now serves divorced, deserted, and never-married individuals and their children. AFDC continues to be the major cash welfare program for families. Federal funds pay at least 50 percent of each state's benefits and administrative costs. In June 1994, enrollment reached 5,028,000 families, just below the record of 5,083,000 set four months earlier. Individual recipients numbered 14.2 million and unemployed two-parent families totaled 362,000. Also, food stamp enrollment in June 1994 was 27.4 million persons—a record high. Although almost half of the mothers who enter AFDC can be expected to leave within two years, most return. Long-term users often are young, never married, and high school dropouts; and most AFDC families begin with a birth to a teenager.

In the past few years, the federal government and state governments have tried to change and improve the welfare system. The Clinton administration campaigned to "end welfare as we know it," though, to date, Congress has not voted on Clinton's loophole-ridden proposal. The administration proposal limits AFDC benefits to two years, during which employment services would be provided to recipients. Nearly twenty welfare reform bills were introduced in the 103rd Congress, including three major proposals offered by Republican members:

**The GOP Leadership Welfare Reform Bill:** After two years on AFDC (or less at a state's option), welfare recipients must work thirty-five hours per week in a private or public sector job. It also requires mothers to establish paternity before receiving AFDC benefits, denies AFDC benefits to parents under age eighteen, and denies increased AFDC benefits for having additional children while on welfare—unless a state enacts laws to exempt itself from any of these requirements.

***The Real Welfare Reform Act:*** This measure prohibits AFDC, food stamps, and public housing to unmarried mothers under age twenty-one (the age limit is raised to twenty-five in 1998); requires that paternity be established as a condition for receiving AFDC, food stamps, and public housing; provides a $1,000 pro-marriage tax credit, requires 50 percent of AFDC recipients to work by 1996; requires single able-bodied food stamp recipients to work for benefits; and freezes the rate of growth in several welfare programs at 3.5 percent per year.

***The Welfare and Teenage Pregnancy Reduction Act:*** This measure freezes AFDC at current funding levels and returns the program to the states in the form of block grants, giving states maximum discretion to design their own welfare-to-work programs. The bill also prohibits AFDC benefits to parents under age eighteen and requires that paternity be established in order to receive AFDC benefits.

Here's what *Contract with America* proposes:

## *Reducing Illegitimacy*

Today, one of every five white children and two of every three African-American children are born out of wedlock. The Personal Responsibility Act is designed to diminish the number of teenage pregnancies and illegitimate births. It prohibits AFDC payments and housing benefits to mothers under age eighteen who give birth to out-of-wedlock children. The state has the option of extending this prohibition to mothers ages eighteen, nineteen, and twenty. The savings generated from this provision to deny AFDC to minor mothers (and to mothers age eighteen to twenty if the state elects that option) is returned to the states in the form of block grants to provide services—but not cash payments—to help these young mothers with illegitimate children. The state will use the funds for programs to reduce out-of-wedlock pregnancies, to promote adoption, to establish and operate children's group homes, to establish and operate residential group homes for unwed mothers, or for any purpose the state deems appropriate. None of the taxpayer funds may be used for abortion services or abortion counseling.

The bill also includes a number of other provisions to reduce illegitimacy. While AFDC is prohibited to mothers ages seventeen and younger who have children out of wedlock, mothers age eighteen who give birth to illegitimate children must live at home in order to receive aid—unless the mother marries the biological father or marries an individual who legally adopts the child. Mothers already receiving AFDC will not receive an increase in benefits if additional children are born out of wedlock.

Finally, the Personal Responsibility Act requires mothers to identify the father as a condition for receiving AFDC. Exceptions are provided for cases of rape and incest and if the state determines that efforts to establish paternity would result in physical danger to the mother. The bill requires states to establish paternity in 90 percent of their cases. Also, states are encouraged to develop procedures in public hospitals and clinics to determine paternity and establish legal procedures that help pinpoint paternity in a reasonable time period.

## Requiring Work

States are allowed to establish their own work training and education programs to help recipients move from the welfare program to paid employment as soon as possible. The training programs require recipients to work for an average of thirty-five hours a week or thirty hours per week plus five hours engaged in job search activities. One parent in a two-parent family is required to work thirty-two hours a week plus eight hours of job searching. States may not provide the work programs for more than two years to any individual or family who receives welfare benefits. States have the option of ending AFDC to families that have been on the welfare rolls for two years, if at least one year was spent in a work program. All states must terminate AFDC payments to families who have received a total of five years of welfare benefits—regardless of whether or not the AFDC recipient has participated in a jobs program.

As long as states meet the participation requirements, the federal government will not meddle in other parts of the program. States will design their own work programs and determine who will be required to participate in them. Part of the participation requirement is requiring a certain number of recipients to participate in the jobs program.

Starting in 1996, 100,000 AFDC recipients will be required to work; in 1997, 200,000 recipients will be required; in 1998, 400,000 will be required; in 1999, 600,000 recipients will be required; in the year 2000, 900,000 will be required; and by 2001, 1.5 million recipients will be required to work.

Identified nonparents, usually men, who receive food stamp benefits are required to work—eight hours per week for those benefits.

### Capping the Growth of Welfare Spending

The Personal Responsibility Act caps the spending growth of AFDC, SSI, and numerous public housing programs, and the mandatory work program established under the bill. The cap equals the amount spent the preceding year for these programs with an adjustment for inflation plus growth in poverty population. The entitlement status of these programs is ended.

The bill also consolidates a number of nutrition programs into a block grant to states, funded in the first year at 95 percent of the total amount of the individual programs. Programs consolidated into the block grant include food stamps, the supplemental feeding program for women, infants, and children (WIC), and the school lunch and breakfast programs, among others. Under the block grant, states will distribute food assistance to economically disadvantaged individuals more freely.

To further reduce welfare spending, welfare assistance (AFDC, SSI, food stamps, housing, and a host of other public assistance) is denied to noncitizens, except refugees over seventy-five years of age, those lawfully admitted to the United States, or those who have resided in the United States for at least five years. Emergency medical assistance will continue to be provided to noncitizens.

## State Flexibility

Recognizing that the best welfare solutions come from the states, not Washington, D.C., the Personal Responsibility Act allows states to create their own work programs and determine who participates in them. States can also opt out of the AFDC program and convert their AFDC payments into a fixed annual block grant and have the option to provide new residents AFDC benefits comparable to the level provided in the state in which they previously resided. To help combat illiteracy, states may reduce AFDC payments by up to $75 per month to mothers under the age of twenty-one who have not completed high school or earned their high school equivalency. Payments may also be reduced if a dependent child does not maintain minimum school attendance.

## Other Provisions

State adoption agencies are encouraged to decrease the amount of time a child must wait to be adopted (today, the average child waits approximately 2.8 years). Specifically, the bill prohibits states from discriminating on the basis of race, color, or national origin when placing children for adoption.

Also, AFDC beneficiaries whom the state identifies as addicted to drugs or alcohol must enroll in an addiction treatment program and participate in random drug testing in order to continue receiving welfare benefits.

## Savings to American Taxpayers

The Personal Responsibility Act is estimated to result in net savings of approximately $40 billion over five years. The denial of welfare to noncitizens saves about $22 billion, the cap on welfare spending saves about $18 billion, the nutrition block grant saves about $11 billion, and the requirement for paternity establishment saves about $2 billion. The costs included in the bill are $9.9 billion for the work program and approximately $2 billion for miscellaneous state options.

## Myths versus Facts

**Myth:** Time limits on AFDC payments are too inflexible to be effective.

**Fact:** This proposal actually gives states more flexibility (we give states the option of ending cash

AFDC payments after two years on the welfare rolls, provided the person spent at least one year in a work program). Republicans believe time limits on welfare benefits must be real limits, not replacing one type of welfare check with another. Government help should be tied to personal responsibility and should not be unending.

**Myth:** Cutting off a meager check for a welfare mom will not deter teen pregnancy.

**Fact:** Republicans understand one important thing ignored by most Democrats—incentives affect behavior. Currently, the federal government provides young girls the following deal: Have an illegitimate baby and taxpayers will guarantee you cash, food stamps, and medical care, plus a host of other benefits. As long as you stay single and don't work, we'll continue giving you benefits worth a minimum of $12,000 per year ($3,000 more than a full-time job paying a minimum wage). It's time to change the incentives and make responsible parenthood the norm and not the exception.

**Myth:** Republican work requirements are inflexible, and they might hurt parents who are least able to work.

**Fact:** The Republican welfare plan is a contract to promote individual responsibility among able-bodied welfare recipients. In 1988, Congress

placed a work requirement on two-parent families—the only such work requirement in all of
federal welfare law. We need to build upon this
work requirement, instead of reduce it, as Bill
Clinton proposes. Unlike all other Democratic
bills, our plan will require 1.5 million AFDC recipients to work by the year 2000.

**Myth:** Placing a cap on welfare spending is a cruel
measure that will put mothers and kids on the
street. We need more flexibility; every welfare
case is different.

**Fact:** The Republican plan is extremely flexible, and
it will save tens of billions of taxpayer dollars—
unlike the President's plan, which would spend
over $9 billion. The fact is, we've spent $3.5 trillion on antipoverty programs since the advent of
President Johnson's Great Society in 1965. Our
bill caps several major welfare programs but adjusts
them for inflation and population. We also end
welfare benefits for noncitizens, with the exception of emergency medical. The federal government now spends at least $7 billion per year to
provide welfare benefits to around 2 million noncitizens. Consolidating the nutritional programs
into one discretionary block grant to the states will
enable them to best deal with their varying needs.

**Myth:** Giving states the option to opt out of the current AFDC program and convert those monies into

fixed annual block grants is just a way to sidestep federal responsibility for the nation's welfare and shift the problem onto individual states.

**Fact:** Even President Clinton has advocated allowing states to be innovative in addressing our nation's welfare problem. Unfortunately, his one-size-fits-all welfare reform bill has failed to match his rhetoric. States and localities are closer to the public than the bureaucrats in Washington, D.C. are. Americans demand action on welfare reform, action like innovative Republican governors such as Tommy Thompson of Wisconsin are taking to reduce the welfare rolls.

# Strengthen Families
# and Protect Our Kids

SHOULDN'T WE DO more to protect and strengthen the American family? The American family is at the very heart of our society. It is through the family that we learn values like responsibility, morality, commitment, and faith. Today it seems the values of the family are under attack from all sides—from the media, from the education establishment, from big government.

Our Family Reinforcement Act is pro-family because it recognizes the value of families. We will strengthen the rights of parents to protect their children against education programs that undermine the values taught in the home. We will crack down on deadbeat parents who avoid child support payments. Pay up, or be forced to work by the state.

Our *Contract with America* protects children by increasing the penalties for assaults against children and by getting tough on child pornography. We will encourage adoption by providing a tax credit to assist families with the high cost of adoption. And our *Contract* helps ease the financial cost of caring for elderly loved ones by creating a tax credit for dependent care.

After forty years of putting government first, Republicans will put families first by voting on the Family Reinforcement Act in the first one hundred days of our majority in the House of Representatives. It's a change long overdue.

## *The Family Reinforcement Act*

The family is the core of American society. It is the principal mechanism through which values, knowledge, discipline, and motivation are passed from one generation to the next. But rather than bolstering the American family, the policies of the Clinton administration undermine it. The Family Reinforcement Act strengthens the rights of parents—rejecting the Democratic Party view that "government knows best."

The Family Reinforcement Act (1) protects parents' rights to supervise their children's participation in any federally funded program and shield them from federally sponsored surveys that involve intrusive questioning; (2) requires states to give "full faith and credit" to child support orders issued by the courts or the administrative procedures of other states; (3) provides a refundable tax credit of up to $5,000 for families adopting a child; (4) strengthens penalties for child pornography and criminal sexual conduct involving minors; and (5) provides a $500 tax credit for families caring for a dependent elderly parent or grandparent.

## *Family Privacy Protection*

The bill requires parental consent for the participation of a minor in any federally funded survey or analysis regarding (1) parental political affiliations; (2) any mental or psychological problems in the family; (3) family or individual sexual behavior and attitudes; (4) any illegal or self-incriminating behavior; (5) privileged relationships with lawyers, physicians, or clergymen; (6) any household income information other than that required by law for federal program participation; (7) religious beliefs; and (8) appraisals of other individuals with whom the minor has had a familial relationship.

### Child Support Enforcement

The Family Reinforcement Act requires states to give "full faith and credit" to child support orders from other states. It provides federal assistance in developing a uniform child support/visitation order in order to streamline interstate enforcement. Finally, the bill requires noncustodial parents who receive state aid to participate in a state job-search program if they owe back child support payments.

### Adoption Assistance

The bill establishes a refundable tax credit of up to $5,000 for adoption expenses such as adoption fees, court costs, and attorney fees to make it easier for families to adopt. The tax credit is phased out for incomes beginning at $60,000.

### Eldercare Assistance

The Family Reinforcement Act aims to keep families intact by providing financial assistance to families who might otherwise have to place parents or grandparents in a nursing home. It provides a $500 tax credit for families caring for a dependent elderly parent or grandparent at home.

## Child Protection

The bill increases sentences for sexual offenses against children and closes certain loopholes in federal laws protecting children. Today, computers with their enhanced graphics and rapid communication are increasingly used by pornographers. To address this, the bill increases federal sentencing guidelines by two levels for the use of a computer in the shipment of pornography.

Current law provides a maximum sentence of ten years for the prostitution of children. The Family Reinforcement Act establishes a three-year minimum sentence for anyone who forces children into prostitution. It also assures that an increase in the age of the victimized child will not result in lighter punishment.

Finally, the bill creates mandatory three-year minimum sentences for sexual abuse of a minor or a minor who is a ward in federal custody. Currently, federal laws are much weaker than most state laws in these areas, and are therefore seldom used. Creating mandatory minimum sentences will reactivate prosecutions under these federal laws.

## Myths versus Facts

**Myth:** Giving parents the right to pick and choose what their children study will lead to chaos in the schools, which will be forced to try to accommodate individual schedules. In addition, forcing schools to adopt a dual system for some programs is unfair to the children who will inevitably be confused about whether they are somehow different than their peers.

**Fact:** Republicans believe parents know what's best for their children—not the government. Schools can accommodate the legitimate needs of students and their parents.

**Myth:** Democrats, not Republicans, have taken the lead on stricter child support enforcement laws.

**Fact:** While President Clinton waited until June 1994 to unveil his costly one-size-fits-all welfare reform plan, Republicans have long advocated a get-tough approach toward parents who evade their responsibilities to their children. For instance, on October 25, 1992, President Bush signed a law making it a federal crime for parents who lived in another state to avoid paying child support. During the 103rd Congress, we had a welfare reform plan on the table that included additional tough provisions that cracked down on deadbeat parents.

**Myth:** Tax incentives for adoption are unnecessary. There are now waiting lists of parents who want to adopt—they need no financial incentives.

**Fact:** All kids should be afforded the opportunity to grow up in a nurturing family. Our proposal will effectively expand the pool of parents to include those who would like to adopt but cannot afford it. The children now needing homes are those who would benefit the most from an expanded pool of adoptive parents.

**Myth:** We don't need a dependent care tax credit for seniors. We need universal health care that provides long-term care benefits to seniors.

**Fact:** Republicans believe that as the family goes, so goes the nation. Strong families and strong communities make a strong America. We don't need a government-run health care system with costly new entitlement programs. Instead, we need to facilitate efforts to keep families intact.

# Tax Cuts for Families

DON'T YOU THINK your tax bill is too high—that you aren't getting what you pay for out of Washington? In 1992, America was promised tax relief for middle-class families. However, the promise of a middle-class tax cut quickly turned into the largest tax increase in American history. In the first one hundred days of a Republican Congress, we will make good where others have failed by voting on the American Dream Restoration Act.

Our *Contract with America* recognizes families for what they are—the basic building block of society. Renewing the American Dream is our goal, and renewing that dream starts at home, with the family. To help families reach their American Dream, our *Contract* calls for $500-per-child tax credit, to make raising children a little more affordable. With this tax credit, a family of four earning $28,000 a year would see their tax burden cut by a third.

Then we'll begin to repeal the marriage tax penalty. The government should reward, not punish, those who enter into the sacred bonds of marriage. And finally we will create American Dream Savings Accounts to make it easier for average Americans to save money, buy a home, pay for medical expenses, and send their kids to college.

Renewing the American Dream is what our *Contract* is all about. By strengthening families, we strengthen America. Here's what we propose:

## *The American Dream Restoration Act*

Bill Clinton promised middle-class tax relief during his campaign for President but instead gave families the biggest tax increase in American history—$275 billion over five years, including higher taxes on gasoline and Social Security benefits that added to the tax burden of the middle class.

The American Dream Restoration Act provides a tax credit for families, reforms the so-called marriage penalty and establishes a new and improved Individual Retirement Account. Today, the average family spends more on taxes than it spends on food, clothing, and shelter combined. Many families now need a second earner not to support the household, but to support the government. Middle-income families are forced to buy their first homes later in life and must scramble to send their children to college. Our act is designed to deliver relief from the heavy burden of government and let families keep more of their hard-earned dollars to pursue their own version of the American Dream.

### *$500 Family Tax Credit*

Effective in 1996, the bill provides a $500-per-child tax credit for families with annual incomes up to $200,000. (A child is defined as an individual under eighteen years of age.) The tax credit will benefit approximately 50 million families, 90 percent of which earn less than $75,000 per year. For example, the tax credit will cut by more than a third the tax burden for a family of four with $28,000 annual income, helping to scale back the heavy tax burden the Clinton Democrats imposed on the American people in 1993.

## Reform of the Marriage Penalty

The 1993 tax increases and expanded Earned Income Tax Credit resulted in many married couples across the income spectrum paying higher taxes than they would by filing as two singles. For example, two single people who each earn $40,000 pay $6,633 each in taxes. Once married, their tax liability leaps to $14,551, or $1,285 more. Our bill would reform the tax code to make it fairer to married couples.

The American Dream Restoration Act provides up to $2 billion annually of marriage penalty relief. Each family currently subject to the marriage penalty would be entitled to a credit determined by the U.S. Secretary of the Treasury.

## Tax-Deductible Individual Retirement Accounts (IRAs)

The American Dream Restoration Act allows individuals to contribute up to $2,000 a year into an American Dream Savings Account. Nonemployed spouses may also participate. The account is "back-ended," meaning the individual pays income taxes on the amount deposited, but not on the amount withdrawn if used for (1) retirement income; (2) purchase of a first-owner occupied home; (3) education expenses at a postsecondary institution (college or training institution) for self, spouse, or dependent child; or (4) medical costs, including purchase of insurance for long-term care.

Within two years of enactment of our bill, current IRA participants can cash out their current IRA and pay the tax due on it without having to pay any penalty provided the money is transferred to an American Dream Savings Account.

## *Myths versus Facts*

**Myth:** This tax credit is just another attempt by the Republicans to serve the interests of their rich friends.

**Fact:** Ninety percent of the families assisted by the $500-per-child tax credit would earn less than $75,000 a year. Families with annual incomes over $200,000 aren't even eligible for the tax credit.

**Myth:** The proposed tax credit would balloon the federal deficit and raise the debt burden on the same children for whom the credit was proposed.

**Fact:** The tax credit would return at least $100 billion in tax money to poor and middle-class Americans over five years. Republican proposed spending cuts would more than cover this cost to the U.S. Treasury.

**Myth:** Cutting taxes for married taxpayers would mean heavier tax burdens on single taxpayers.

**Fact:** Single taxpayers would not face higher taxes. Republican proposed spending cuts would more than offset the tax revenue lost by reforming the marriage penalty. Fairness dictates that taxpayers be treated equally, whether married or single.

**Myth:** The Republicans' so-called American Dream Savings Account wouldn't benefit the average American. You have to be rich to realize any benefits.

**Fact:** Both middle-class and poor Americans would benefit from expanded Individual Retirement Accounts. Anyone who pays taxes—anyone with an income—would benefit by being able to set aside a small but significant sum of money each year to cover post-secondary education expenses, a first-time home purchase, medical expenses, and retirement. With IRA contributions limited to just $2,000 annually, this proposal is designed to benefit the average American.

**Myth:** This proposal would generate large budget deficits and pressure the Congress to raise taxes and cut important spending programs.

**Fact:** This proposal would have very little impact on the budget deficit, but a very important impact on the lives of the average American taxpayers. As a nest egg from which to draw, these American Dream Savings Accounts represent opportunities for more and better education, home ownership, medical security, and retirement without the fear of poverty. Further, as an incentive to save, these American Dream Savings Accounts would provide this country with more capital with which to invest in America's future.

# Strong National Defense

ISN'T NATIONAL DEFENSE the first and foremost priority of the federal government? For forty years prior to the fall of the Berlin Wall, Americans stood shoulder to shoulder against international communism—and we won. But with the end of the Cold War, some have taken to raiding the defense budget to fund social welfare programs and UN peacekeeping programs. Our defense forces have been cut so deeply that we risk a return to the "hollow military" of the 1970s. And for the first time in our history, American troops have been placed under UN command.

A Republican House of Representatives will change this by voting on the National Security Restoration Act within our first one hundred days. Our *Contract with America* includes a vote to stop putting American troops under UN command; to stop raiding the defense budget to finance social programs and UN peacekeeping; and to stop gutting Ronald Reagan's vision of protecting America against nuclear or chemical attack. Republicans are committed to a defense against missile attacks from terrorist states such as North Korea, Iran, and Libya.

Providing for the common defense is the first duty of our government. It is not optional. With Republicans in the majority, we will stop undermining our military and give Americans security with peace of mind.

Here's what we'll do:

## *The National Security Restoration Act*

The National Security Restoration Act reforms the Department of Defense to ensure that U.S. troops are only deployed to support missions in America's national security interests, to reinvigorate a national missile defense, and to accelerate the expansion of NATO. Other provisions in the bill are designed to address concerns that readiness has suffered because defense spending has been cut too far and too quickly in order to pay for expensive social programs.

U.S. defense spending as a percentage of gross domestic product, is at its lowest level since World War II, and many assert that any more military reductions could leave us unprepared to respond to unforeseen global threats. Despite severe personnel reductions and shortfalls in funding over the last ten years, American troops have been deployed more often and have taken part in more operations per year than ever before. Currently, over 48,000 U.S. personnel serve in unstable regions such as Haiti, Iraq, Bosnia, Macedonia, the Adriatic Sea, Rwanda, and the Caribbean.

The National Security Restoration Act addresses this problem by:

• restricting the Defense Department from taking part in military operations that would place U.S. troops under foreign command;

• requiring an accurate and comprehensive review of U.S. defense needs by authorizing a blue-ribbon panel of independent defense experts to assess military readiness, maintenance practices, and general operational needs;

- restoring defense spending "firewalls" that prohibit the transfer of Defense Department funds to other departments and agencies in order to fund social spending programs unrelated to military readiness. Future defense spending cuts are to be used only for deficit reduction;

- renewing America's commitment to an effective national missile defense by requiring the Defense Department to deploy antiballistic missile systems capable of defending the United States against ballistic missile attacks; and

- renewing our commitment to a strong North Atlantic Treaty Organization (NATO) by urging the Clinton administration to proceed with full NATO partnership discussions with nations that are striving to embrace democracy, enact free market economic reforms, and place their armies under civilian control.

## Background

*Bottom-up Review:* In 1990–91, the Bush administration studied how U.S. military forces should be restructured after the end of the Cold War and produced a blueprint for a base force 20 to 25 percent smaller in budget and forces than the current structure. In spite of this review, the Clinton administration decided to undertake its own "bottom-up review"—making its own assessment of the country's post–Cold War defense needs and making its own proposals to restructure the military to meet them. In September 1993, the bottom-up review was released with its recommendation to cut an additional 10 percent on top of the Bush administration proposals. The FY 1995–99 defense spending recommendation was $91 billion below the Bush administration's adjusted baseline of $1.3 trillion and $13 billion more than the Clinton administration's own defense spending target of $1.2 trillion. Defense Secretary Les Aspin expressed the administration's intent to trim down spending to meet the target. The FY 1995 defense authorization bill was the first defense authorization measure drafted in accordance with the bottom-up review.

The review's proposals are based on maintaining a force structure sufficient to win two major regional conflicts simultaneously (a strategy called win-win). The review claims savings of (1) $24 billion from cutting 160,000 more active duty personnel than the Bush administration; (2) $19 billion from infrastructure changes, including base closings, and cutting 115,000 more civilian personnel than the Bush administration; (3) $21 billion from realigning ballistic missile defense programs; and (4) $32 billion from reduced development and procurement of many systems. Savings were also achieved in weapons modernization programs.

The Clinton administration argues that the review's force structure reflects a cautious strategy to maintain U.S. freedom of action in a still dangerous world. The U.S. military will have greater strategic mobility, more firepower, and be armed with "smart" and "brilliant" weapons. Moreover, additional savings will be possible from changes in strategic nuclear programs and minor procurement programs, acquisition reform, and Vice President Al Gore's national performance review.

Critics have charged that (1) the win-win strategy is purely military—that is, the Clinton administration has yet to develop a national security strategy encompassing all its concerns and priorities; (2) the proposed force is inadequate; it is the same force that previous Defense Department analyses considered appropriate for less demanding strategies; (3) the strategy overestimates the savings to be achieved from base closures; (4) the bottom-up review force cannot be maintained within the Clinton administration's own budget guidelines; (5) the Army, with only ten active divisions, will be hard-pressed to support the win-win strategy while fulfilling peacekeeping missions around the globe; (6) cutting the aircraft carrier fleet from thirteen to eleven will create gaps in global coverage; and (7) the Air Force may have too few long-range attack aircraft, too few aerial tankers, and an insufficient airlift capacity to support two major regional conflicts.

## The Current Outlook for Defense Spending

***President Clinton's FY 1995 Defense Budget Request:*** On February 7, 1994, President Clinton presented his FY 1995 defense budget to Congress. Recommending $263.7 billion, the Clinton administration's budget plan continues the decline in military spending that began in the late 1980s. Under the President's proposal, by FY 1997, the budget for national defense will fall to about 40 percent of the FY 1985 spending peak (in constant, inflation-adjusted dollars), with spending beginning to level off after that.

Late in 1993, discussion of the defense budget focused on a five-year $50 billion gap between the projected cost of planned military programs and the amount available under existing budget plans. The projected gap was mainly due to higher estimates of inflation and a congressionally mandated military pay raise. Subsequently, revised inflation estimates reduced the projected gap, and the President approved an increase of $11.4 billion over five years in defense funding to cover costs of the pay raise. These changes narrowed the gap to about $20 billion, but the administration decided to postpone dealing with the shortfall until 1994.

Following debate on the defense funding shortfall, the President reaffirmed support for his long-term defense spending plan by arguing in his State of the Union address against further cuts. Perhaps partly because of the President's endorsement of the defense plan, debate over defense spending levels was relatively muted once the House and Senate considered the annual congressional budget resolution in March 1994. In the House, a proposal to reduce FY 1995 defense budget authority by $2.4 billion was defeated by a substantial margin. But both chambers also rejected proposals to increase five-year defense spending levels by at least the $20 billion shortfall. The Senate approved a measure to reduce caps on overall discretionary spending by $46 billion in the budget authority and $26 billion in outlays. Although many supporters of the measure argued that the cuts should not come from defense, critics warned that the Defense Department would likely bear a large share of the reductions. The House, which had no comparable provision, narrowly rejected a motion to instruct conferees to include these Senate-passed cuts, and the final conference agreement split the difference between the House and the Senate, cutting $13 billion in outlays over five years. The allocation of the reductions was left to the appropriations committees.

Debate over the FY 1995 defense budget was heated, focusing on a number of longer-term defense spending and policy issues, including whether the administration budget is sufficient to maintain high levels of military readiness, whether the planned military force is large enough to support the military strategy articulated in the bottom-up review, and whether the necessary pace of weapons modernization will outrun likely weapons budgets after the turn of the century.

## Spending Trends

Over the past several years, debate has focused not on whether defense spending should be cut, but rather by how much. Proponents of greater and accelerated reductions have argued that with the end of the Cold War, funds previously allocated for defense are now free to be spent on urgent domestic needs. With defense spending currently at its lowest level (as a percentage of GDP) since World War II, others have argued that downsizing must be done methodically and carefully, warning that quick and deep reductions in the past have left the United States unprepared to respond to unforeseen global threats.

A key issue in the current defense policy debate is whether the defense budget projected by the Clinton administration for the next several years is sufficient to support a well-equipped, well-trained, high-quality military force. Defense analysts have generally assumed that if the size of the military force remains stable, then defense spending will and probably should grow moderately over time in order to purchase and operate more modern equipment and to improve the quality of life in the military. Some observers see current defense budgets as comparable (in inflation-adjusted prices) to average Cold War–era budgets, and conclude that a continuing "Cold War level of funding" should suffice to support a substantially smaller, post–Cold War force. Because defense spending normally has grown over time relative to the size of the force, however, such a comparison may not be very meaningful. When the normal growth in defense funding per troop is taken into account, it appears that currently planned budgets will begin to fall below the historical trend over the next few years. How well or how poorly the budget fits the force will depend on the impact of a slowdown in weapons modernization and on how well efforts to protect readiness are managed. Senior administration officials acknowledge that procurement funding has declined substantially in recent years, but this is acceptable in the short run, they say. Judging by historical standards, however, significant increases in defense funding may be necessary in the future to maintain a capable force of the planned size unless there are significant changes in patterns of acquisition and operations.

## International Peacekeeping Operations

The United States participates in a number of peacekeeping operations worldwide, most of which are organized, carried out, and paid for by America in association with UN efforts. Currently, the incremental costs associated with the mission—costs above and beyond normal peacetime operating expenses—are funded through (1) supplemental appropriations, (2) Defense Department reprogramming, (3) absorption by Defense Department accounts, and (4) earmarkings in annual defense funding bills. The United States has thirteen ongoing missions. In 1993, President Clinton requested $597 million for peacekeeping and Congress appropriated $401.6 million. Because of the rapid increase in both the number and cost of peacekeeping operations since the end of the Cold War, some members of Congress have expressed concern about the existing funding procedures. One solution is to create a new account to hold advanced funding of U.S. peacekeeping missions. The Clinton administration tried to do this in the FY 1994 defense budget, calling the account the Global Cooperative Initiative, but it was rejected by Congress.

The United States also funds peacekeeping operations through mandatory contributions to the UN.

The United States is responsible for 25 percent of the UN's normal operating budget and 31.7 percent of the cost of each UN-sponsored peacekeeping activity. The peacekeeping assessment was raised from 30.4 percent to 31.7 percent last year to compensate for reduced contributions by the now-dissolved Soviet Union. This increase added fire to existing concerns about the UN's management practices, causing the administration to demand that the U.S. share be reduced to 25 percent.

At the end of the Cold War, partially fueled by the success of Operation Desert Storm, enthusiasm for peacekeeping operations peaked. But the mood quickly changed as Americans monitored an inconclusive U.S. mission in Somalia and considered the possibility of many American deaths in a ground war in Bosnia. On May 8, 1994, the Clinton administration unveiled criteria the President will use to decide which peacekeeping efforts to support with money, troops, or both. Under these criteria, in order for the United States to vote in favor of a mission it must advance U.S. interests; result from a threat to international peace and security; and have clear, realistic objectives. The criteria for deciding whether to commit troops to the mission, especially if combat is expected, are more stringent. The directive also makes clear that American forces can never be placed under foreign command unless doing so would serve American security interests. White House National Security Adviser Anthony Lake describes these guidelines as an attempt to reform and limit U.S. participation for such activities.

Here's what our *Contract with America* proposes:

## Restricting Multinational and UN Command of U.S. Troops

***Prohibition of Foreign Command of U.S. Armed Forces:*** We would prohibit the Defense Department from taking part in military operations that place U.S. troops under foreign command. The President may waive this provision if he certifies to Congress that operational control of our troops under foreign command is vital to our national security interests. No later than ten days after this certification, the President must report to Congress with (1) a description of the vital national security interest that requires the placement of U.S. troops under foreign command; (2) the size, composition, mission, and objectives of the U.S. troops involved and the estimated time the troops will serve under foreign command; (3) the U.S.'s cost for the mission; (4) the precise command-and-control relationship between the United States and the foreign command structure; and (5) the extent to which the U.S. troops will rely on non-U.S. military forces for security and self-defense and an assessment of those forces' ability to carry out these duties.

***Placing U.S. Troops Under Foreign Command for U.N. Peacekeeping Activities:*** The bill stipulates that any special peacekeeping agreement negotiated between the President and the UN Security Council that places U.S. troops under foreign command must be approved by Congress. The President may not place U.S. troops under foreign command unless he (1) reports to Congress with the size, composition, mission, and command structure of U.S. troops involved; (2) certifies that placing U.S. troops under foreign command is vital to national security; (3) retains the option to remove U.S. troops from peacekeeping activities at any time; and (4) guarantees that all U.S. troops placed under foreign leadership will remain under American administrative command for discipline and evaluation. The above stipulations must be met no less than fifteen days before U.S. troops are placed under foreign command.

**Notice to Congress of Proposed UN Peacekeeping Activities:** The President must report to Congress at least fifteen days prior to any UN Security Council vote authorizing UN peacekeeping activities that involve the use of U.S. troops and funds. The report is to include a description of U.S. force involvement, the mission of the U.S. troops, the cost and source of funding for our share of the mission, and an estimated termination date for troop involvement.

**Transmittal to Congress of UN Resolutions and Reports:** Within twenty-four hours after the UN Security Council adopts a resolution authorizing peacekeeping activities involving U.S. troops, the President must submit the text and supporting documentation of the resolution to Congress.

**Reports to Congress on U.S. Contributions for UN Peacekeeping Activities:** The President must (1) notify Congress within fifteen days after the United

Nations submits a billing statement to the United States for its share of peacekeeping activities, and (2) notify Congress at least fifteen days prior to disbursing funds for peacekeeping.

***Budgeting for Annual U.S. Contributions for UN Peacekeeping Activities:*** The President is directed to submit to Congress, along with his annual budget, a report with estimates of the U.S.'s fiscal year funding requirements for UN peacekeeping. Beginning with the FY 1996 budget, the President is to submit to Congress an estimate of all U.S. costs associated with UN peacekeeping for each of FY 1996, 1997, and 1998.

***Annual Reports to Congress on Peacekeeping:*** No later than ninety days after enactment, and each year thereafter at the time of the President's annual budget submission, the President is to report to Congress on U.S. contributions to UN peacekeeping. The report is to include (1) the number and nature of ongoing peacekeeping activities, (2) the priority and anticipated duration of each ongoing activity, (3) an assessment of each ongoing peacekeeping operation and its effect on U.S. national security, (4) the total costs of each UN peacekeeping mission and the U.S. contribution to each of these missions, and (5) an assessment of UN management of peacekeeping activities. The initial report is to include the costs for all UN peacekeeping activities since October 1945. Subsequent reports are to include the same information for the preceding and current fiscal year.

*U.S. Reimbursement for In-Kind Contributions to UN Peacekeeping Operations:* Beginning in FY 1995, appropriated peacekeeping funds may not be used to pay the U.S. share of UN operations unless the Defense Department certifies to Congress that the UN has reimbursed the Department for all goods and services that have been provided to the UN on a reimbursable basis.

*Limitation on the Use of Defense Department Funds For UN Peacekeeping:* Beginning October 1, 1995, Defense Department Operations and Maintenance funds for U.S. contributions to UN peacekeeping missions are subject to congressional authorization.

*Assessed Contributions for UN Peacekeeping Activities:* The bill expresses the sense of Congress that (1) the United States should not fund more than 25 percent of the total cost of any UN peacekeeping mission, and (2) the UN should review each nation's assessed contributions for UN peacekeeping activities.

*Buy America Requirement:* No U.S. funds may be contributed to the UN for peacekeeping activities unless the Secretary of State determines that U.S. manufacturers and suppliers are being given the opportunity to provide equipment, services, and material for peacekeeping mission activities equivalent to those being given to foreign manufacturers and suppliers.

***U.S. Personnel Taken Prisoner While Serving in Multilateral Peacekeeping Missions:*** The bill expresses the sense of Congress that the President should take all necessary steps to (1) ensure that any U.S. military personnel captured during UN peacekeeping activities are to be treated as prisoners of war and (2) bring to justice all individuals responsible for the mistreatment, torture, and death of American prisoners.

***Provision of Intelligence to the UN:*** The United States is authorized to provide intelligence assets to the United Nations only if the President and the secretary general of the UN agree to the types of intelligence to be provided, the circumstances under which the intelligence assistance is to be provided, and the procedures to be observed by the UN to ensure the secrecy of the intelligence. The President must report to Congress at least thirty days prior to entering into such an agreement.

***UN Peacekeeping Budgetary and Management Reform:*** The bill contains numerous budgetary reforms to ensure efficiency when the United States contributes funds to the UN. At the beginning of each fiscal year (beginning in FY 1995), 50 percent of all U.S. funds made available for UN peacekeeping must be withheld until the President certifies to Congress that (1) the UN has established an independent and objective Office of Inspector General to audit, inspect, and investigate peacekeeping activities; and (2) the secretary general of the UN has appointed an inspector general who is proficient in accounting, financial analysis, law, and public administration.

### Comprehensive Review of U.S. Defense Needs

**Independent Blue-Ribbon Panel:** The bill establishes a blue-ribbon panel to conduct an accurate and comprehensive review of America's national security needs, force readiness requirements, and modernization plans. This provision comes in response to critics of President Clinton's bottom-up review who assert that it contained unrealistic financing for the established goals.

### Restoring Budget Firewalls for Defense Spending

The bill stipulates that Defense Department funds may not be transferred to any other department or agency unless the Secretary of Defense reports to Congress, at least thirty days before these funds are to be made available, with proof that it is vital to U.S. national security interests. The Defense Department may waive this provision during periods of national emergency declared by the President or Congress; however, the waiver may not take effect until Congress has been notified.

## Renewed Commitment to a National Missile Defense

The Defense Department is directed to (1) develop for deployment at the earliest possible date a cost-effective, operational antiballistic missile defense system to protect the United States against ballistic missile threats (for example, accidental or unauthorized launches or Third World attacks); (2) implement as quickly as possible advanced theater missile defense systems; and (3) report to Congress within sixty days of enactment with a plan for both missile defense systems.

## Renewed Commitment to a Strong North Atlantic Treaty Organization (NATO)

On January 10, 1994, leaders of the NATO member nations meeting in Brussels issued an invitation to European countries that do not belong to NATO to participate in the Partnership for Peace program. In that invitation, NATO reaffirmed its commitment to expand the organization to increase the security of the North Atlantic area. NATO pointed out that many European countries that in the past had been adversaries, had rejected ideological hostility to the West and, in varying degrees, had begun to implement policies aimed at achieving democracy, protecting human rights, and building free-market economies.

The bill expresses the sense of Congress that (1) the United States should continue its commitment to an active leadership in NATO; (2) the United States should join with its NATO allies to redefine the alliance's role in the post–Cold War world (taking into account the changes in central and eastern Europe and the emerging security threats posed by nuclear, chemical, and biological weapons of mass destruction); (3) the United States should reaffirm that NATO military planning includes joint military operations outside of NATO jurisdiction; (4) that Poland, Hungary, the Czech Republic, and Slovakia should be in a position to further the principles of the North Atlantic Treaty and contribute to the security of the North Atlantic area no later than January 10, 1999 (the bill also states that these countries should continue working toward democracy, free-market economies, and civilian control of their militaries); (5) the United States should assist these nations as they work toward inclusion in NATO; and (6) other European nations should be invited to join NATO in the future if they agree to contribute to the security of the North Atlantic.

The President is given authority to establish a program to assist Poland, Hungary, the Czech Republic, Slovakia, and other European countries that are working toward full membership in NATO. The program is to assist the new nations with joint planning and military exercises with NATO forces and encourage greater interoperability of military equipment to achieve a uniform military doctrine. The President may also provide assistance to other European countries emerging from communist domination if he certifies that they have made significant progress in embracing democracy and establishing free-market economies.

## President's Report to Congress

Within one year after enactment, and at least once every year thereafter, the President is to report to Congress on the progress made by Poland, Hungary, the Czech Republic, Slovakia, and other emerging European countries in their efforts to achieve full NATO membership.

## Myths versus Facts

**Myth:** President Bush used multilateralism and the UN to defeat Iraq; President Clinton is simply following that tradition when he uses multilateralism and the UN to rescue Haiti and continue the relief operation in Somalia. The Bush administration supported a UN-based New World Order; the Clinton administration is putting that policy into practice.

**Fact:** The Bush administration did not advocate that American forces be placed under UN command. The Clinton administration appears to salute the day when American men and women will fight, and die, "in the service" of the United Nations. President Clinton has not led great coalitions of countries, as did George Bush of Desert Storm or Dwight Eisenhower of D-Day. Instead, he either asks the UN permission *first* before defending American interests, *or* uses its token support to mask the tragic international adventurism of his administration.

**Myth:** The Clinton administration inherited an anti-quated Reagan-Bush defense establishment geared toward fighting the Cold War with the former Soviet Union. Through the bottom-up review, the administration analyzed, for the first time, the legitimate security needs of the United States in a post–Cold War world and crafted a defense program that meets those needs.

**Fact:** Virtually nobody, not even the Secretary of Defense, defends the current funding levels of the defense budget. Furthermore, many even question whether the administration has told the American people the truth about its defense strategy. When *The New York Times* (on September 15, 1994) complains that "it did not take long for the Pentagon's 'bottom-up review' to bottom out," all Americans should be concerned about the defenses of the United States. The Pentagon itself calculates that the budgetary shortfall will exceed $40 billion over the next five years. The GAO, which did an independent study, found the Clinton defense program underfunded by $150 billion over five years.

**Myth:** The Clinton administration is not raiding the defense budget to pay for expanded social spending programs. Under Presidents Reagan and Bush, social programs, which genuinely helped the needy, were raided to pay for a bloated defense budget that was not needed. The Soviet Union would have collapsed under the weight of its own inefficiencies without the United States spending trillions of dollars on weapons systems that it will never use. The American people are now entitled to a peace dividend and budget priorities that puts them first, not the military.

**Fact:** President Clinton has enacted the largest tax increase in U.S. history and increased social programs in excess of $100 billion. Still, by all accounts, the defense budget is inadequately funded. Since defense spending is clearly the only part of the budget that the Clinton administration has seriously cut, a balanced approach to budget cuts has to be maintained as it was under the Bush administration. Consequently, so-called firewalls must be erected to ensure that the lives of American soldiers are not jeopardized in order to pay for dubious social programs such as midnight basketball and the like. If the armed forces are being asked to do more with less, the Clinton administration must use their sacrifice to reduce the budget deficit.

**Myth:** The Reagan administration overstated the usefulness of the Strategic Defense Initiative and jeopardized U.S. relations with the Soviet Union. The Clinton administration is simply placing "Star Wars" within the overall defense priorities of the United States in the new post–Cold War world. It is important to American interests that hardliners in Russia are not inflamed by the United States abandoning the Anti-Ballistic Missile Treaty signed by Republican President Richard M. Nixon.

**Fact:** The Clinton administration has, for the first time, extended Russian veto powers over American strategic defenses, going against the wishes of the Joint Chiefs of Staff. Although the Cold War is supposed to be over, the Russians want the United States to freeze its expanding capability in high-speed antimissile defenses at current technology levels. To do this, they want America to continue to observe the ABM Treaty, which was signed by the Soviet Union and United States in 1972. This treaty is a Cold War relic that does not meet the future defense needs of the United States when a number of potentially hostile countries will possess nuclear weapons and ballistic missile technology. We are being asked to limit our defenses against the entire world. It is a moral imperative that U.S. strategic defenses be expanded and that the Clinton administration not yield to Russian demands that Americans remain defenseless in the face of potential nuclear aggression—no matter from what quarter it may come.

**Myth:** The Republicans just don't get it: The Cold War is over. The old divisions in Europe must be transcended so all European nations are brought within a new NATO-based collective security system, called the "Partnership for Peace." To include Poland, Hungary, and the Czech Republic in an old NATO alignment against Russia would only plant new divisions over old ones. Lines should not be drawn in Europe. It is time that Republicans stopped being paranoid of Russia.

**Fact:** Russia has no need to be threatened by Poland, Hungary, and the Czech Republic joining NATO unless Russia still harbors imperial designs on Europe. However, the countries of eastern Europe know only too well what Russia is capable of doing, under czar and commissar alike. Those countries in Europe that meet the criteria of democratic elections, free markets, and civilian control of the military should be allowed to join NATO. Russia still has to prove that it will observe its new boundaries, which goes against its centuries-old imperial tradition and the beliefs of many within its military and government. It is in the interest of the United States to expand eastward the frontier of freedom in Europe. We should not ask Moscow for permission first, as the Clinton administration does.

# *Fairness for Senior Citizens*

DON'T SENIOR CITIZENS deserve a break rather than a tax hike? Americans today are living longer and reaching their retirement years in better health than ever before. Our senior citizens have taken this great nation through incredible years, and we owe them a tremendous debt of gratitude. Too many seniors are now facing effective marginal tax rates of more than 50 percent, a rate much higher than that of other Americans. That is why our *Contract with America* calls for the repeal of 1993's tax increase on Social Security benefits. And for those between the ages of sixty-five and sixty-nine, we will raise the Social Security earnings limit three-fold—to $30,000—so they may continue working if they choose. Washington should not be in the business of driving productive seniors out of the job market.

We also call for tax incentives to help older Americans purchase long-term care insurance, so they can better afford the high health care costs that may come in the later years of life.

Senior citizens are threatened every day by bigger government, higher inflation, and higher taxes. We will address these problems in our first hundred days by voting on the Senior Citizens' Equity Act. Our *Contract* treats seniors with the respect they deserve, and we offer positive solutions to help those who have given so much, and who have made us the great nation we are today. Here's what we'll do:

## *The Senior Citizens' Equity Act*

Every year more Americans join the ranks of the elderly. Our tax laws, however, impose harsh penalties on our senior citizens, especially those who continue to work beyond age sixty-five. The Social Security Earnings Limit pushes millions of seniors out of the work force and 1993's tax hike on Social Security benefits hit 6.1 million middle-income seniors. On top of these financial burdens, many seniors worry about being able to take care of their long-term health care needs.

The Senior Citizens' Equity Act removes financial burdens on American senior citizens to (1) allow them to earn more income without losing Social Security benefits and (2) reduce the percentage of Social Security benefits on which they must pay taxes to the level before they were increased by the Clinton administration in 1993. The bill provides tax incentives to encourage individuals to buy private long-term care insurance and makes it easier for seniors to reserve retirement communities for adults only without facing lawsuits.

## *Background*

Americans over the age of sixty-five number more than 30 million and constitute more than 12 percent of the population. Two important areas of concern for them are Social Security and the cost of long-term care.

## The Social Security Earnings Test

Congress passed the Social Security Act in 1935 as part of President Franklin D. Roosevelt's New Deal, establishing a program to provide income to older Americans. The program has always included an earnings test. There have been many proposals to alter or end the earnings test, but none has been enacted. Social Security benefits are intended to compensate for income lost because of retirement, but many seniors have complained that it is unfair to punish those who keep working by not allowing them to collect Social Security benefits when they have paid into the system all of their working lives.

## Social Security Benefits Tax

The other provision of the bill affecting Social Security deals with a relatively new phenomenon. Social Security benefits were not taxed at all until 1984. It was then that a system was established whereby individuals with total income of $25,000 or more and couples with a total income of $32,000 or more would have to pay taxes on up to 50 percent of their Social Security benefits. In 1993, President Clinton sought to tax up to 85 percent of these individuals's Social Security benefits. Although the House approved this provision as part of the 1993 Omnibus Budget Reconciliation bill, the provision was modified in conference. The final version of the bill increased the maximum percentage of benefits that could be taxed to 85 percent, but also created a second set of thresholds at $34,000 for individuals and $44,000 for couples. The bill created a complicated system whereby recipients who had to pay taxes on 50 percent of benefits continue to do so, and those whose income exceeds the new threshold have to pay taxes on up to 85 percent of benefits.

## Long-Term Care

The cost of long-term care concerns senior citizens and others. About 7.1 million of the elderly need long-term care, and estimates indicate 13.8 million may need it by 2030. Most long-term care is paid for by private individuals and Medicaid. Many elderly do not need constant medical attention, but do need assistance with daily activities. Medicare and most other health insurance plans do not cover most services associated with long-term care. In order to qualify for Medicaid assistance for long-term care, individuals must first spend a significant portion of their own savings and other assets.

## Increase of the Social Security Earnings Limit Threshold

Under current law, senior citizens between the ages of 65 and 69 lose one dollar in Social Security benefits for every three dollars they earn above $11,160. This earnings test amounts to an additional 33 percent marginal tax rate, on top of existing income taxes, and punishes seniors who choose to remain productive beyond age sixty-four. Over five years, our bill would raise to $30,000 the amount seniors can earn before losing Social Security benefits. The limit will be raised according to the following schedule:

—By January 1, 1996 seniors can earn $15,000 without losing Social Security benefits.
—By January 1, 1997, $19,000.
—By January 1, 1998, $23,000.
—By January 1, 1999, $27,000.
—By January 1, 2000, $30,000.

## Repeal of Clinton's Social Security Benefits Tax

The 1993 Omnibus Reconciliation Act requires senior citizens who earn more than $34,000 (singles) or $44,000 (couples) to pay income taxes on 85 percent of their Social Security benefits. Over five years, our bill would return the amount of Social Security benefits subject to income tax to 50 percent, the level of benefits taxable before the 1993 Omnibus Reconciliation Act. The percentage of Social Security benefits subject to income taxes will drop from 85 percent to: 75 percent for tax year 1996, 65 percent for tax year 1996, 60 percent for tax year 1997, 55 percent for tax year 1999, and 50 percent for tax year 2000.

## Tax Incentives for Private Long-Term Care Insurance

Our bill includes several provisions pertaining to the tax treatment of long-term health care included in the Affordable Health Care Now Act, the House Republican health reform package:

• allows tax-free withdrawals from IRAs, 401(k) plans, and other qualified pension plans in order to purchase long-term care insurance;

• allows accelerated death benefits to be paid from life insurance policies for individuals who are terminally ill or permanently confined to a nursing home; and

• treats long-term care insurance as a tax-free fringe benefit and the same as accident and health insurance for taxation purposes.

The bill also allows deductions for long-term care premiums, limited to the following amounts (indexed for inflation annually):

| | |
|---|---|
| Age 40 and under | $200 |
| Age 40 to 50 | $375 |
| Age 50 to 60 | $750 |
| Age 60 to 70 | $1,600 |
| Age 70 and older | $2,000 |

### *Senior Citizen Retirement Communities*

Current law is vague on what constitutes senior housing. Consequently, lawsuits have been brought against real estate agents and retirement community board members. Our bill allows housing communities to meet the Fair Housing Amendments Act's "adults-only housing test" if those communities can prove that at least 80 percent of their units have occupants age fifty-five or older.

The Fair Housing Amendments Act of 1988 prohibits discrimination based on familial status, although it does include a vague definition of adults-only housing. Under current law, senior communities are exempt from the 1988 law's antidiscrimination provisions if at least 80 percent of the units in a senior community are occupied by those fifty-five and over, and the community has "significant facilities" such as support rails and transportation vans. The law, however, does not specifically state what must be present to merit exemption.

This current vague definition has posed problems for many retirement communities and has resulted in lawsuits against real estate agents and retirement community board members. This provision of our bill repeals the significant facilities test and exempts real estate agents and community board members from liability for monetary damages in lawsuits if they acted on a good-faith belief that the community was exempt. Thus, senior communities must only meet the 80 percent test to be awarded an exemption.

### *Myths versus Facts*

**Myth:** Increasing the Social Security earnings limit threshold would allow wealthy seniors to become even more wealthy, while retaining their Social Security benefits.

**Fact:** During the presidential campaign, even candidate Bill Clinton promised he'd "lift the Social Security earnings test limitation so that older Americans are able to help build our economy and create a better future for all." Republicans believe the earnings penalty discriminates against our senior citizens and hurts our economy because it prevents us from being able to benefit from the talents of thousands of experienced professionals. If the President is sincere, he will join our effort to ease this burden on seniors.

**Myth:** Repealing the $25 billion Social Security tax increase of 1993 would increase the deficit and send a message to wealthy seniors that they can continue to live on the government gravy train.

**Fact:** Evidently President Clinton and the Democratic Congress believe $34,000 is the national threshold of great wealth. Republicans want to provide tax relief to middle-class seniors by restoring the law as it stood prior to Clinton's 1993 tax-and-spend measure.

**Myth:** Tinkering with the tax code is no way to provide long-term care benefits to the elderly. We need universal health care with long-term care benefits.

**Fact:** Placing the entire health-care system under the control of politicians as the Clintons propose would undermine the security of senior citizens who have made responsible financial decisions and taken steps to retain their access to health care. Instead, we need to pass legislation that would help individuals afford long-term nursing home and home health insurance coverage—without creating an expensive, government-run program that will bust the budget.

# Roll Back Government Regulations and Create Jobs

ISN'T IT TIME we got Washington off our backs? Too many people in Washington believe that government is the only solution to our problems. When it comes to creating jobs, government is more often the problem rather than the solution. The small economic recovery that started in 1992 is in danger of dying because of high taxes and reams of new regulations that stifle productivity. By voting on the Job Creation and Wage Enhancement Act in the first one hundred days of a Republican House majority, we will begin to remake our economy into the greatest job growth machine in the world.

Our *Contract with America* includes provisions to roll back taxes on investments that create jobs and modernize factories. And our *Contract* helps small businesses—the heart and soul of our economy. To free Americans from bureaucratic red tape, we will require every new regulation to stand a new test: Does it provide benefits worth the cost?

To help our cities and states—the government closest to you—we will ban unfunded mandates that threaten to bankrupt many local communities. And to protect individual Americans from overzealous federal regulators, we will make sure that private property cannot be taken away without just compensation.

Renewing the American Dream requires a growing economy that provides hope for the future. Our *Contract with America* encourages and promotes the entrepreneurial spirit which has made us the most blessed nation on earth.

Here's what we propose:

## The Job Creation and Wage Enhancement Act

Republicans favor lower taxes on the investment that creates jobs and the income people derive from jobs. In order to support more government programs and their bureaucracies, the Democrats have consistently advocated high taxes on both income and capital. Republicans also favor cost-effective regulations to address real risks. Democrats have worked hard to prevent analysis of government regulations to determine their real contribution to our common welfare. For example, the Clean Air Act expressly forbids agencies from weighing economic effects in writing their implementing regulations.

The burden of taxes and regulation on investment created an economic "growth gap" between the historic post–World War II rate of 4 percent real growth per year to a projection of only 2.5 percent real growth through the end of this century. Cutting taxes on investment and savings will spur greater job creation, and slashing federal red tape will increase worker wages.

The Job Creation and Wage Enhancement Act includes a variety of tax-law changes and federal bureaucratic reforms designed to enhance private property rights and economic liberty and make government more accountable for the burdens it imposes on American workers. Specifically, the bill:

• provides a 50 percent capital gains rate cut and prospectively indexes capital gains to account for inflation;

• increases the value of investment depreciation to equal the full value of original investment;

• allows small businesses to deduct the first $25,000 worth of investment each year;

• clarifies the home office deduction;

• empowers taxpayers to designate a portion of their tax liability to a public debt reduction fund;

• requires federal agencies to assess the risk and cost of each imposed regulation;

• forces federal agencies to publicly announce the cost of their policies;

• requires Congress to report the cost of mandates it imposes on state and local governments;

• reduces the paperwork burden imposed on American business 5 percent;

• limits the government's ability to impose undue burdens on private property owners; and

- requires federal agencies to complete regulatory impact analyses.

Government-imposed mandates and regulations suppress wages and excessive taxation of capital and investment stifles economic growth and job creation. Current federal policies threaten the competitiveness of American business, stifle entrepreneurial activity, and suppress economic growth and job creation. Regulations can also have a direct impact on the lives of all Americans—raising the prices they pay for goods and services, restricting the use of their private property, and limiting the availability of credit. The Job Creation and Wage Enhancement Act lowers taxes on investment and reins in regulation to create additional jobs, enhance wages, and recognize private property rights.

Supporters assert it is consistent with the maintenance of a competitive marketplace that is committed to breaking down unnecessary barriers to entry created by regulations, statutes, and judicial decisions. The Job Creation and Wage Enhancement Act calls for open, simultaneous, and immediate competition within all industries in the United States.

### Capital Gains Tax Cut

The Job Creation and Wage Enhancement Act allows individuals to exclude from taxes 50 percent of capital gains income, effectively halving the rate. Under the legislation, individuals in the 15 percent income tax bracket would pay an effective capital gains tax rate of 7.5 percent, those in the 28 percent bracket would effectively pay 14 percent, and those in the top bracket of 39.6 percent would pay 19.8 percent on capital gains. Corporations would pay a 17.5 percent capital gains rate. In addition, individuals may deduct any capital loss with respect to the sale or exchange of a principal residence.

The bill indexes the basis of capital assets for inflation (prospectively) so taxes are not paid on illusory earnings. Democratic Party class war rhetoric to the contrary, sound economic analysis indicates that 92 percent of the after-tax benefits of lower taxes on capital goes to wage earners, not investors.

## Neutral Cost Recovery

The Job Creation and Wage Enhancement Act increases the value of investment depreciation to equal the full value of the original investment. Under current law, the present value of investment depreciation is less than the full cost of the original investment because the amounts deducted in later years are eroded by inflation and opportunity cost.

This change in law would dramatically increase jobs and economic growth. An analysis by the Institute for Policy Innovation projected that the proposal would create 2.7 million jobs, produce an additional $3.5 trillion in economic activity by the year 2000, increase the U.S. gross domestic product by $1 trillion annually, and increase economic activity by 1.8 percent annually.

## Small Business Appreciation

In the economic expansion of the Reagan years, small businesses accounted for about 12 million of the 18 million new jobs added to the economy. The Clinton administration has pounded Main Street with an unrelenting stream of new mandates, taxes and regulations and our bill would provide much-needed relief.

The Job Creation and Wage Enhancement Act recognizes the important contribution small businesses make in our economy by encouraging investment and alleviating the cumbersome paperwork of depreciation schedules. Its provisions include:

• raising the expensing level from $17,500 to $25,000, allowing small businesses to deduct the first $25,000 they invest in equipment and inventory each year;

• clarifying the home office deduction, allowing taxpayers to qualify if the home-office is (1) used exclusively for business purposes, (2) used on a regular basis, (3) used to perform tasks that could not easily be performed elsewhere, and (4) is essential to the taxpayer's business; and

• increasing the estate tax exemption from $600,000 to $750,000, thus restoring the value eroded by inflation and making it easier for small business owners and family farmers to keep their shops and farms in the family.

## *Taxpayer Debt Buydown*

The national debt currently exceeds $3.5 trillion, and each year Congress adds to the debt, spending billions more than it takes in. The Job Creation and Wage Enhancement Act allows taxpayers to designate up to 10 percent of their tax liability to be used to help reduce the public debt. The designated funds would be transferred to the Public Debt Reduction Trust Fund to be established by the Department of Treasury. Congress is required to reduce spending equivalent to the amount designated by the taxpayer. If for some reason the spending cuts do not occur, an across-the-board sequester will be imposed on all government accounts except the Federal Deposit Insurance Corporation, the National Credit Union Administration, and the Resolution Trust Corporation.

## *Risk Assessment/Cost Benefit Analysis*

Congress is never forced to ensure that the benefits of regulation, better health and productivity, outweigh the costs, lost jobs, and lower wages. Nor does Congress pursue integrated health and safety goals. Instead, Congress and federal regulators often attack whatever health risk has caught the public's attention, even if its regulatory solution exacerbates other health risks.

The Job Creation and Wage Enhancement Act requires each federal agency to assess the risks to human health and safety and the environment for each new regulation. Agencies must also provide the cost associated with the regulation and an analysis comparing the economic and compliance costs of the regulation to the public. Each agency must form an independent peer review panel to certify the assessment and incorporate the best available scientific data. The review panel members must either possess professional experience conducting risk assessment or in the given field of study.

### Regulatory Budget

Today's budget deficit is high on the public policy agenda because it is easily measured and understood. American families can't spend more than they take in, and Congress should live within those same rules. Congress finds its way around Americans' dislike for taxes and deficits by simply forcing American businesses and workers to carry out federal mandates and regulations. The cost of the regulations is no different than a tax—but it doesn't show up in the federal budget, and families don't feel it on tax day, April 15.

The bill requires federal agencies to issue an annual report projecting the cost to the private sector of compliance with all federal regulations. The cost of the regulations will then be capped below its current level forcing agencies to (1) find more cost-effective ways to reach goals and (2) identify regulatory policies whose benefits exceed their costs to the private sector.

## Unfunded Mandate Reform

The Congressional Budget Office has estimated that the cumulative cost of new regulations imposed on state and local governments between 1983 and 1990 is between $8.9 billion and $12.7 billion. That cost is paid by every taxpaying American. Unfunded federal mandates remove the ability of state and local governments to direct their tax dollars toward the communities' established priorities. They also impose one-size-fits-all policies on areas as diverse as New York City and rural Iowa. State and local governments resort to higher taxes to meet the costs of unfunded federal mandates.

The bill requires the Congressional Budget Office to issue an analysis of each piece of legislation containing a federal mandate (a program that burdens state and local governments with undue costs resulting in over $5 million annually). The analysis must include a description of the mandate, the expected cost to state and local governments, and if the mandates are to be partly or entirely unfunded. CBO budgetary impact reports are to be printed in the committee reports accompanying legislation. The bill caps the mandates cost below its level for the preceding year.

## Strengthen Paperwork Reduction Act and the Regulatory Flexibility Act

Compliance with federal regulations consumes tens of thousands of man-hours annually. Employers must hire lawyers and other experts to fill out the government paperwork. Consequently, they hire fewer workers to produce goods and services. To address this problem, the Job Creation and Wage Enhancement Act requires the government to reduce the paperwork burden by five percent annually. Also, it subjects the Regulatory Flexibility Act to judicial review, so small businesses can sue to enforce the law. The Regulatory Flexibility Act determines whether or not a regulation has a substantial impact on a significant number of small businesses.

### Protection Against Federal Regulatory Abuse

The bill provides individuals with a "Citizens' Bill of Rights" when being inspected or investigated by a federal agency. The bill of rights affirms an individual's rights to (1) remain silent, (2) refuse a warrantless search, (3) be warned that statements can be used against them, (4) have an attorney or accountant present, (5) be present at an inspection or investigation, and (6) be reimbursed for unreasonable damages. Also, the Job Creation and Wage Enhancement Act allows individuals who are threatened by a prohibited regulatory practice to take legal action against the responsible agency. A prohibited regulatory practice is defined as an inconsistent application of any law, rule, or regulation causing mismanagement of agency resources by any agency or employee of the agency.

### Private Property

The Job Creation and Wage Enhancement Act allows private property owners to receive compensation (up to 10 percent of fair market value) from the federal government for any reduction in the value of their property. If a question arises over the value of the property, the private property owner may use an arbitrator to decide the outcome.

## *Regulatory Impact Analysis*

The bill requires federal agencies to complete a regulatory impact analysis when drafting a major rule (affecting more than a hundred people and costing more than $1 million). The bill lists 23 specific criteria the agencies must follow, including; (1) explaining the necessity and appropriateness of the rule, (2) a statement of whether the rule is in accord with or in conflict with any legal precedent, (3) a demonstration that the rule is cost-effective, (4) an estimate of the number of persons affected by the rule, and (5) an estimate of the costs to the agency for implementation of the rule.

## *Myths versus Facts*

**Myth:** Reducing the capital gains tax unfairly benefits the rich at the expense of the poor and middle class.

**Fact:** A capital gains tax reduction would spur economic growth to the benefit of the rich, poor, and middle class alike. Sound economic analysis demonstrates that 92 percent of the after-tax benefits of lower taxes on capital goes to wage earners, not investors.

**Myth:** Cutting the capital gains tax would reduce federal tax revenue and expand the size of the federal budget deficit.

**Fact:** Unrealized capital gains produce no capital gains tax revenues. As previous history has shown, reducing the capital gains tax rate stimulates realizations and produces more capital gains tax revenue than you would have generated had you not reduced the rate. Further, through its positive impact on the overall economy, a reduction in the capital gains tax rate would raise total federal revenue above what it would have otherwise been.

**Myth:** Neutral cost recovery is just another costly tax loophole for big business.

**Fact:** Prosperity tomorrow demands investment today in productive capacity, new technologies, and human capital. Federal tax policy influences business decisions—including decisions on investment in structures and equipment. The current tax provisions are biased against long-term business investment. Since neutral cost recovery would allow businesses to depreciate full 100 percent of the purchase price of their investments, businesses could be expected to invest more heavily. Investment today means jobs and prosperity tomorrow.

**Myth:** Neutral cost recovery would cost the U.S. Treasury billions of dollars in lost tax revenue.

**Fact:** Not true. Neutral cost recovery would reinvigorate the U.S. economy and generate more tax revenue than was "lost." According to the Institute for Policy Innovation, the Republican proposal would create 2.7 million jobs, produce an additional $3.5 trillion in economic activity by the year 2000, increase U.S. gross domestic product by $1 trillion annually, and increase economic activity by 1.8 percent annually.

**Myth:** Taxpayer empowerment to reduce the budget deficit and the national debt is nothing but a gimmick.

**Fact:** This will allow taxpayers the opportunity to take personal involvement in deficit reduction. This is a participatory control on spending.

**Myth:** Taxpayer empowerment to reduce the budget deficit and the national debt will lead to massive increases in the federal income tax.

**Fact:** In fiscal year 1995 the federal government will collect approximately $595 billion from individual income taxes. This proposal would allow taxpayers to earmark up to $59.5 billion of that sum for the federal debt buydown initiative. Congressional Republicans have repeatedly offered proposals cutting in excess of $60 billion from the federal budget. Democrats who aren't willing to cut $60 billion from a $1.5 trillion budget must not sincerely care about constraining the budget deficit or the growth of big government. Forced to establish more definitive spending priorities, Congress would reduce both the budget deficit and the costs of interest on the national debt.

**Myth:** The buydown initiative would gut national defense spending and leave the country with a Jimmy Carteresque "hollow military."

**Fact:** Republicans have repeatedly offered budget proposals that cut billions from the federal budget without slashing defense spending to dangerous levels. It is, in fact, the Clinton administration that has already gutted national defense spending. President Clinton's most recent budget proposal reduces FY95 budget authority for defense procurement (purchase of bullets, tanks, ships, et cetera) 36 percent below 1977 levels (remember how underfunded the military was during the late 1970s) and 68 percent below 1985 levels. Moreover, the Clinton FY95 budget reduces budget authority for military personnel 14 percent below 1977 levels and 26 percent below 1985 levels. Defense spending need not face additional cuts.

**Myth:** This would be unfair to lower income Americans. They earn less and therefore would have less influence over the fiscal policy of the federal government. This would give the rich a disproportionate ability to slash spending and save themselves from progressive tax increases.

**Fact:** The vast majority of income taxes in this country are paid by ordinary working families—if anyone should have disproportionate influence, it is this group of taxpayers.

**Myth:** Cost-benefit analysis would cause people to die.

**Fact:** Cost-benefit analysis would save lives. Cost-benefit analysis would allow regulators to optimize the use of their resources. For example, rather than consume $1 billion in resources to save ten lives, cost-benefit analysis would inform regulators how to reallocate those same resources to save more than ten lives.

**Myth:** Processes for controlling the growth of regulation are inherently antiregulation.

**Fact:** The objective is not to cause a certain level of regulatory burden, but to make the regulatory burden a matter of conscious choice rather than of accident. It is a matter of restoring government accountability.

**Myth:** Since regulatory costs are inherently arbitrary, a regulatory budget would be highly vulnerable to political gamesmanship.

**Fact:** Requiring that costs be calculated and considered when imposing regulations would actually add an objective guide and more accountability to what is now an out-of-control process.

**Myth:** The costs associated with unfunded mandates are difficult to measure.

**Fact:** Many unfunded mandates are quite easily calculable. Just ask the state and local officials who must find the funds to pay them.

**Myth:** These provisions state mere goals. These desired outcomes cannot be legislated into existence simply because they are desired.

**Fact:** Goals provide direction. Without them, government becomes rudderless and progress becomes a hit-or-miss proposition.

**Myth:** Government should focus on the problems facing the average American, not on trying to reduce the paperwork burden by 5 percent.

**Fact:** Paperwork imposes costs. Unnecessary paperwork imposes unnecessary costs. Since these costs come at the expense of the average American, we ought to do everything possible to minimize them.

**Myth:** This is nothing more than an attempt to undermine necessary regulations.

**Fact:** No, this is an attempt to comply with the Bill of Rights. According to the Fifth Amendment, "nor shall private property be taken for public use, without just compensation." Having lived under arbitrary, tyrannical government, the Founding Fathers knew this to be a matter of liberty and simple fairness.

**Myth:** A process of regulatory impact analysis would be vulnerable to political influences. Imagine what would happen if the Republicans were able to use this process to reverse all of the environmental progress made over the past two decades.

**Fact:** Many government regulations do far more harm than good. They were drafted for political reasons and they continue to exist for political reasons. Implementing a system of regulatory impact analysis would provide greater accountability and guard against the creation of more politically motivated regulations. Government exists to serve everyone, not the interest of a special few.

# Common Sense Legal Reforms

ISN'T IT TIME to clean up the court system? Frivolous lawsuits and outlandish damage rewards make a mockery of our civil justice system. Americans spend an estimated $300 billion a year in needlessly higher prices for products and services as a result of excessive legal costs. The delays and costs caused by legal abuses put the legal system out of reach for average Americans.

Our *Contract with America* includes a package of common sense legal reforms that will put justice back in our civil justice system. Within the first hundred days of a Republican House, we will vote on the Common Sense Legal Reforms Act.

Our bill penalizes frivolous lawsuits by making the loser pick up the winner's legal fees, and it imposes mandatory penalties on lawyers who abuse the system. It curbs the use of "junk science" in court and requires so-called experts to be real experts. It helps lower prices by curbing abuses in product liability, stopping runaway punitive damages, and by directing legal blame at only those responsible for the injury. With our package of common sense legal reforms, we can eliminate excessive costs and long delays and we can restore fairness to the American court system. The time has come. Here's how:

## *The Common Sense Legal Reforms Act*

Our legal system has become burdened with excessive costs and long delays, and no longer serves to expedite justice or ensure fair results. Instead, overuse and abuse of the legal system impose tremendous costs upon American society. It has been estimated that each year the United States spends some $300 billion as an indirect cost of the civil justice system. In fact, in 1989 alone, 18 million civil lawsuits were filed in state and federal courts—amounting to one lawsuit for every ten adults. Although the vast majority of these cases are filed in state courts, federal reforms can have a substantial impact and provide a model for state reform, without having reform dictated to the state by Washington.

The Common Sense Legal Reforms Act does many things, including making sure that expert witness testimony is based on scientifically sound evidence, that product liability laws are uniformly applied, that abusive securities lawsuits are limited, and that opportunities for alternative dispute resolution are expanded.

## *Background*

Almost everyone agrees that America has become a litigious society: We sue each other too often and too easily. In the federal courts alone, the number of lawsuits filed each year has almost tripled in the last thirty years—from approximately 90,000 in 1960 to more than 250,000 in 1990. As President Bush's Council on Competitiveness found, this dramatic growth in litigation carries high costs for the American economy: manufacturers withdraw products from the market, discontinue product research, reduce their workforces, and raise their prices.

In addition to the sheer volume of lawsuits that filter through the legal system each year are the problems associated with frivolous suits. In many cases, defendants know that the suit would not stand on its own merits, but agree to settle out of court just to avoid the endless and expensive claim and appeal processes. Such responses merely perpetuate our propensity to sue. Legal experts point to a few straightforward reforms that can help stem abuse of the system. Promoting voluntary settlements instead of court trials and encouraging meritorious claims while discouraging baseless suits and devious trial tactics are just some of these proposals.

## Loser-Pays Rule

The Common Sense Legal Reforms Act applies the so-called loser-pays rule (in which the unsuccessful party in a suit pays the attorneys' fees of the prevailing party) to diversity cases filed in federal court. A diversity case involves citizens from different states. However, the bill limits the size of the coverage to the loser's own attorneys' fees costs (for example, if the prevailing party spent $100 defending himself and the unsuccessful party spent $50, then the unsuccessful party is responsible for only $50 of the prevailing party's court costs). Courts may also impose other limits on the award of attorneys' fees.

The loser-pays rule strongly discourages the filing of weak cases as well as encourages the pursuit of strong cases, since claimants can get their court costs reimbursed if they win.

Many lawsuits could be avoided if the parties would just sit down and discuss their differences before going to court. To achieve this first common sense step, the bill requires claimants to notify the other party prior to filing suit, thus encouraging settlements before resorting to litigation.

### Honesty in Evidence

The last decade has witnessed an explosion of abusive practices involving rent-an-expert-witnesses and unsupported scientific theories. So-called experts too often base their opinions on "junk science" in order to justify absurd claims.

The Common Sense Legal Reforms Act amends Rule 702 of the Federal Rules of Evidence regarding expert witness testimony to state that expert testimony is not admissible in a federal court (1) unless it is based on "scientifically valid reasoning" and (2) if the expert is paid a contingency fee (however, the bill allows the judge to waive this second prohibition).

### Product Liability

The legislation creates a uniform product liability law (covering state and federal actions) in three areas: punitive damages, joint and several liability, and fault-based liability for product sellers.

It is news to no one that juries have been out of control over the past decade in awarding punitive damages far in excess of what is recovered to make a plaintiff whole. Part of the blame is to rest on the system, because it gives juries very little guidance with which to make such awards.

For punitive damages, the bill requires that claimants establish by "clear and convincing evidence" that the harm they suffered was the direct result of malicious conduct. Under the measure, punitive damages are limited to three times the actual harm (i.e., the economic damages awarded). For claimants with little actual harm, awards of up to $250,000 could be awarded.

The Common Sense Legal Reforms Act also abolishes joint liability for noneconomic losses (mental distress, pain and suffering, et cetera) and holds defendants liable for only their own portion of the harm. Under current law, a defendant can be held responsible for the entire award even if he is not completely responsible for all the harm done. For example, if a consumer sues the manufacturer, the buyer, the shipper, and the merchant and only the merchant is solvent, the merchant becomes responsible for the total amount of damages awarded by the court—including the portions owed by the other parties. The solvent individual is then forced to recover the others' portions on his own. This legislation would make an individual party responsible for only the portion of damages directly attributable to it.

Finally, the bill makes product sellers liable only for harms caused by their own negligence (for example, altering or assembling a product or making false claims about the product). Product sellers would be responsible for manufacturer errors only when the manufacturer cannot be brought to court or lacks the money to pay a settlement.

### Attorney Accountability

Attorneys often operate under a billing arrangement, called a contingency fee, that is based on a percentage of the damages recovered. While this fee arrangement helps some worthy claimants have access to the courts, it also creates a situation ripe for abuse by attorneys.

The Common Sense Legal Reforms Act expresses the sense of Congress that states should enact laws requiring attorneys practicing within their borders to disclose certain information to clients. Specifically, in contingency fee cases, states should make attorneys disclose (1) the actual duties performed for each client and (2) the precise number of hours actually spent performing these duties.

The bill also amends Rule 11 of the Federal Rules of Civil Procedure to restore the mandatory requirement that courts sanction attorneys for improper actions and frivolous arguments intended to harass, unnecessarily delay, and needlessly increase the cost of litigation. Sanctions are to be determined by the judge and may involve financial penalties, contempt orders, limits on discovery, and other procedural penalties. Prior to December 1, 1993, federal courts were required to impose sanctions for violations of Rule 11. However, on that date the Federal Judicial Conference's recommendations to amend Rule 11 (making sanctions optional rather than mandatory) took effect, since Congress did not act on the proposed rule change.

In addition to reinstating the mandatory sanction, the bill requires, for the first time, that sanctioned attorneys compensate injured parties.

### Prior Notice

At least thirty days before a plaintiff can bring a suit, he must transmit written notice to the defendant of the specific claims involved and the actual amount of damages sought. Proponents of the legislation argue that prior notice of a grievance provides an opportunity for both parties to resolve the dispute without going to court.

### Legislative Checklist

This section of the bill is designed to limit needless and costly litigation resulting from poorly drafted legislation. Frequently Congress fails to directly address basic issues that later result in court challenges. For example, during consideration of the most recent amendments to the Civil Rights Act, Congress failed to resolve the issue of retroactivity. Litigation dragged on for two years until the Supreme Court ruled that the law was not retroactive. This might have been avoided if Congress had been forced to take a decisive stand on the issue.

Our bill seeks to limit such situations by requiring that committee reports address the following issues: preemptive effect, retroactive effect, authorization for private suits, and applicability to the federal government.

## Strike Lawsuits

The Common Sense Legal Reforms Act changes federal securities law to limit so-called strike lawsuits—lawsuits filed by class-action attorneys on behalf of shareholders whose once-attractive stock purchases have failed to live up to their expectations. Although these suits claim that the holding company misrepresented the healthiness of their stocks, many times the downturn can be blamed only on market volatility.

These cases usually involve highly speculative investments in the securities field (less than one percent involve truly fraudulent companies), and it is the attorney, not the shareholder, that benefits from the suit. Since class-action lawyers can make decisions that are not in the best interest of the clients without fear of reprisal and take a big chunk of the settlement off the top, shareholders are often exploited. Strike suits are money-makers for the lawyers, but such frivolous claims destroy jobs and hurt the economy. Instead of spending money on research and development or hiring more employees or reducing the cost of their products, companies end up spending big bucks on strike suit insurance and legal fees. High technology, biotechnology, and other growth companies are hardest hit because their stocks are naturally volatile. Small- and medium-sized companies alone have paid out nearly $500 million during the last two years (settling a case is often times cheaper and quicker than defending in court). The problem is rapidly getting worse: in the last five years, the number of strike suits has tripled.

To address these abuses, the Common Sense Legal Reforms Act (1) provides a court-appointed trustee for plaintiffs (to make sure that lawyers act in the best interests of their clients), (2) guarantees plaintiffs full disclosure of key settlement terms (including a breakdown of how much is to go to them and how much to their lawyers to pay legal fees), (3) limits "professional plaintiffs" to five class-action lawsuits every three years (these individuals typically purchase one share of every stock on the New York Stock Exchange and wait for the stock to drop. They then work with the class-action lawyer to initiate the class action and receive bonus payments for their cooperation), (4) makes losing litigants responsible for the winner's costs, (5) prohibits application of the Racketeer Influence and Corrupt Organizations (RICO) Act to securities cases, and (6) prohibits vague and open-ended complaints. In a key reform, the bill requires that claimants show they relied on intentionally misrepresented information or omissions of information in deciding to purchase their stock, and that their losses were not caused by bad luck in the stock market.

### Myths versus Facts

**Myth:** The "loser pays" approach will discourage the poor and other people who cannot afford to pay for all legal fees incurred from coming forward. The threat of losing will intimidate the poor more than it will the wealthy.

**Fact:** The loser-pays rule seeks to empower plaintiffs with options to litigate their case as they see fit. No plaintiff will be compelled to bring their case under the federal loser-pays rule. Plaintiffs have the *option* of bringing cases under *state* jurisdiction (where the vast majority are not subject to loser-pays rules) or *federal* jurisdiction (where they would be subject to loser pays). The heart of the loser-pays rule seeks to discourage cases without merit. Requiring reimbursement to the prevailing party encourages both sides to evaluate carefully their claims and defenses. It actually *increases access* to the civil justice system to people without resources. Plaintiffs who have a strong case but find the cost of litigation prohibitive can be reassured that the loser will pay the winning party's legal fees. The proposed legislation also discourages the use of a "frivolous defense"—a time-consuming strategy used by clients who can afford exorbitant legal fees to wear down the plaintiff and his or her ability to pay for a lengthy court process. Compensation can also be limited by judicial discretion where appropriate.

**Myth:** The proposed reforms regarding expert witnesses will prohibit the introduction of new theories and studies important to a case. If the expert witness and his or her testimony is not credible, simple cross-examination will expose this. The proposed legislation also denies expert witnesses from being compensated for their time and effort.

**Fact:** These reforms are designed to eliminate testimony that is far afield from mainstream professional practice or current scientific knowledge. The proposed reforms do not discourage legitimate avenues for those who seek expert testimony in order to help judge and jury resolve complex cases. Currently, "expert" witnesses are permitted to offer testimony even if their theories are not proven and are not corroborated by other experts. These witnesses often fool juries and even some attorneys who must accept their testimony as fact—after all, that is why these witnesses are called "experts." Such witnesses regularly offer their "scientific" opinions on the connections between automobile accidents and breast cancer or environmental pollutants and "chemically induced AIDS." Moreover, an expert witness should have no financial interest in any outcome of a case in which he or she testifies. The proposed reforms are designed to keep expert witnesses from becoming mercenaries or advocates, instead of remaining impartial and objective.

**Myth:** The proposed reforms unfairly restrict the amount of damages plaintiffs may receive and denies them just compensation for harm done to them. The reforms also benefit the largest and most wealthy companies—smaller businesses are much more likely to feel the sting of the cost of punitive damages than a large company. If the punitive damages are limited to only three times compensatory damages, there is no incentive for companies who can more easily afford these costs to change their behavior to keep others from being injured.

**Fact:** The Common Sense Legal Reforms Act seeks to prohibit the civil justice system from becoming a "lottery" for plaintiffs, distributing awards in a random and capricious manner. These reforms reduce the threat of runaway jury verdicts, promote settlements, and promote certainty in commercial transactions by establishing reasonable boundaries for awards. Because larger companies service a far larger number of customers, in the aggregate they face greater exposure than do smaller firms. To the extent that the threat of punitive damages is used to positively modify corporate behavior, even under a punitive damage cap, large and small companies face equivalent incentives.

**Myth:** The proposed legislation seeks to restrict attorneys' freedom to contract and places biased restrictions on trial attorneys' income.

**Fact:** The Common Sense Legal Reforms Act seeks to make attorneys accountable for the time and effort they put into specific cases by requiring disclosure of terms of billing arrangement. While contingency fees assist plaintiffs without resources to find attorneys who will benefit only if damages are recovered, they often pay too much. Attorneys can spend a minimal amount of time on open-and-shut cases and reap large rewards from unsuspecting plaintiffs. As officers of the court, attorneys have privileges ordinary citizens do not have. With these privileges go responsibilities. It is not too much to ask that they be honest with their clients.

**Myth:** Mandating a checklist for every piece of legislation passed is simply a Republican gimmick that will end up creating more red tape.

**Fact:** The *Contract* seeks to hold Congress accountable for their actions, insuring that all legislation produced is done out in the open, with all ramifications considered. Too frequently, poor drafting leaves routine areas of the law (statute of limitations or standards of proof) unaddressed. These ambiguities and omissions result in uncertainty and inevitably end up in protracted court challenges that could have been avoided.

# Congressional Term Limits

ISN'T IT TIME we sent the professional politicians a message—that politics shouldn't be a lifetime job? The Founding Fathers envisioned a legislature account-able to the people—a citizen legislature—not a "House of Lords" entrenched in Washington and removed from the concerns of the very people who elect them.

Today, instead of constituents choosing their Con-gressman, too often Congressmen choose their con-stituents in districts gerrymandered to protect the elite power structure of the last forty years. The now-defeated Democratic Speaker of the House sues his own state to block the voters' call for term limits. Yet lawsuits or not, the term limits movement is sweep-ing the nation, and eight out of ten Americans sup-port the idea.

The Democrats won't even debate the issue of term limits. We will. Our *Contract with America* will guaran-tee the first ever vote on a constitutional amendment for term limits. Within the first one hundred days of a Republican House of Representatives, we will vote on the Citizen Legislature Act.

The strength of the grass-roots term-limits move-ment comes from the fact that Washington is simply out of touch with middle America. But we are listen-ing. We hear you. Our *Contract with America* is the agenda of the American people, not of the establish-ment in Washington.

Here's what we propose:

## The Citizen Legislature Act

The Citizen Legislature Act includes a vote on two different term-limits amendments in the first hundred days of a Republican-controlled House. The first would limit the terms of representatives to six years and senators to twelve. The second would impose limits of twelve years in both the House and Senate. Enactment of either would replace career politicians with citizen legislators.

## Background

The idea of limiting the tenure of elected officials has recurred through our history, but it has become more popular in the last few years. In 1992, fourteen states passed initiatives limiting the tenure of federal legislators. Two of these laws, however, have been challenged and found unconstitutional in court. The U.S. Supreme Court will review the ruling by the Arkansas Supreme Court. Since there is a chance the high court will uphold the state court's ruling, a constitutional amendment may be necessary to limit congressional tenure.

House Republicans respect the rights of the states and respect the rights of citizens to limit the terms of their elected officials. In contrast, the Democratic Speaker of the House, defeated in the November 1994 elections, has filed suit against the voters of Washington state to stop the term-limits initiative they passed two years ago. We believe an issue the magnitude of term limits deserves a national debate.

Over the past decade, the rate of reelection for House incumbents was 90 percent. In 1992, the so-called year of change, the reelection rate for incumbents was 93 percent. Such numbers do not represent a citizen legislature as envisioned by the Founding Fathers, but rather a body of government with almost identical turnover to that of Britain's House of Lords, whose members are appointed for life.

An entrenched body of politicians erodes Congress's accountability and responsiveness. An enormous national debt, deficit spending, and political scandals are but a few of the results. Although enacting term limits would not be a panacea, it will be the first step to putting our legislative system back on track.

Term limits have won in every state where the issue has been placed on the ballot—with average victory margins of two to one. Poll after poll reveals strong support for term limits among the American people; a *Wall Street Journal*/NBC News poll found that 80 percent of Americans favor term limits.

The Citizen Legislature Act provides for consideration of two joint resolutions which propose amendments to the Constitution limiting the number of terms members of the Senate and the House of Representatives can serve. The first joint resolution limits the number of Senate terms to two and the number of House terms to six. The second joint resolution also limits senators to two terms, but it limits members of the House to three terms.

## *Myths versus Facts*

**Myth:** It is hypocritical of Republicans who have been in Congress for decades to now claim to be in favor of a "citizen legislature."

**Fact:** The Founding Fathers wanted a true "citizen legislature" with members debating and enacting laws that they would then turn around and live under themselves. It would be unthinkable for them to imagine full-time politicians. It took over a hundred years for the average tenure of a House member to exceed twelve years. Term limits will effectively return Congress to a citizen legislature and act as a check on the misuse of power by members of Congress.

**Myth:** There is already high turnover in Congress; limiting voters' choice is not needed to change the makeup of Congress. For example, in 1992 alone, 25 percent of the House's membership changed.

**Fact:** The reelection rate for members of Congress averaged over 90 percent for all election cycles in the past two decades. In 1992, it was 93 percent. Members of the leadership have been in office for decades. The average tenure of the leadership (committee chairmen and the Speaker, Majority Leader, and Whip) is twenty-seven years.

**Myth:** Term limits restrict the choices available to voters. Voters should be able to vote for anybody meeting basic constitutional requirements. Voters can fire their representatives every two years or reelect anyone whom they believe is performing well.

**Fact:** Choice is already effectively taken away from many voters by the power of incumbency and the entrenched special interests reinforcing these incumbents. Each member receives nearly $1 million in franked mail, staff salaries, and travel expenses every year. In 1992, according to the Heritage Foundation, House challengers raised only 28 cents to every dollar incumbents took in. Term limits would open up the field of candidates—not restrict them. California passed term limits in 1990 for state legislators, and by the 1992 election had a 40 percent increase in candidates running for office.

# Questions and Answers

**With Bill Clinton as President, how will Contract with America *ever become law?***

Both the House of Representatives and the Senate are now under Republican control. Republicans can drive policy and give Bill Clinton an opportunity to govern the way he campaigned for President in 1992—as a New Democrat. When the House and Senate pass a middle-class tax cut, a balanced budget amendment, and a real welfare reform bill, it will be very difficult for President Clinton to veto them.

**Isn't Contract with America *a publicity stunt that is typical of politicians?***

Absolutely not. House Republicans understand why the public is cynical toward Washington and does not trust Congress. Republicans also understand that both parties have been responsible in the past for breaking promises. That is why we have signed the *Contract with America*. It is more than a campaign promise. We have gone the extra mile in laying out our agenda before the whole country. If we fail to keep our word, we'll deserve to be punished. But we will keep our word. At the end of the first hundred days, the American people will understand that House Republicans are different. We want to regain the trust that has been lost over the last several years.

*How do you plan to accomplish all these things in one hundred days when it has taken President Clinton two years and he still has not passed health care?*

One simple difference—our agenda is supported by the vast majority of the American people. President Clinton is trying to pass an agenda that is largely hostile to the needs of most Americans. Our agenda— pro-family tax reforms, regulatory relief, proposals to boost economic growth and job creation, simplifying our legal system to end costly and frivolous lawsuits, real reform of Congress, and many other reforms—is composed of common sense changes that Americans want and need.

The House Republican majority will all be sworn in on January 3, 1995, and will go to work immediately on January 4. Do not expect to see Congress taking any long breaks until the nation's work is done. When the hundred-day agenda is complete, Congress will recess to plan the second hundred-day agenda.

*How will* Contract with America *affect individual Americans?*

In many ways. First, our pro-family tax reforms include a $500-per-child tax credit—so that's $500 more in your pocket for each child—and we'll end the marriage tax penalty that costs many married couples well over $1,000 each year just because they are married. Also, we'll establish American Dream Savings Accounts, which are similar to Super IRAs, where both spouses can invest up to $2,000 each to go into special savings accounts where the interest will never be taxed. The proceeds can be used for the first-time purchase of a home, medical expenses, education expenses, or retirement.

The economic growth reforms will create jobs; legal reforms will cut down on frivolous lawsuits; regulatory reform will make it easier to start and run a small business or family farm; our tough and real crime provisions will keep violent criminals locked up; and we'll make real reforms in Congress to make the institution more accountable to the people.

The American people also want to have faith again in their government and elected officials. Having a Congress that is doing what the American people want and doing it in a way that instills trust will have a strong personal impact on every American.

### What if I disagree with parts of the Contract with America agenda?

Not every Republican or every Democrat will agree on every item. However, the ideas in the *Contract* are shared by the vast majority of the American people, and even if you disagree with one or two of the items, the American people deserve at least to have a national debate and votes on all of these issues.

***Why are House Republicans promising the Contract with America will come to a vote, but not promising its passage? Isn't that disingenuous?***

We are very confident that most of the agenda items will pass. Some of the items are constitutional amendments, which take a two-thirds vote in both the House and Senate to pass. Republicans are making a solemn commitment to bring these bills to a vote, work them aggressively, and, with the help of the American people, they can be passed. This is a two-way *Contract*. The American people are being asked to join the fight in order to pass these common-sense reforms.

***Why did Republican candidates stand on the steps of the U.S. Capitol to sign the* Contract with America*? Doesn't that show they have already become a part of the Washington establishment and thus part of the problem?***

The Capitol once stood as a shining example for the entire world of free people governing themselves. Republicans want to return that trust to the American people. For more than forty years, the Democrats ran Congress with an iron fist, ruining the tradition and trust created by our Founding Fathers. Republicans have taken this responsibility seriously, and want to prove to the American people that our system of government can work as intended, with free people responsibly governing themselves. By standing on the steps of the Capitol, we show respect for the brilliance and genius of the Founding Fathers and great congressional leaders in history.

**Are there issues not in the Contract with America *that may be considered more important to the American people?***

The agenda House Republicans have started with reflects the common desires of a large number of Americans. Not all the candidates or the public agree on all the issues in the *Contract*. But they agree that they need a voice and they need a vote. There will be more opportunities to debate other issues. As the majority party, Republicans will have more than this hundred-day window to bring issues to a full hearing in the House of Representatives.

***If* Contract with America *is about opening up the legislative process, does that mean Republicans will allow a Democratic agenda to come up for a vote?***

Republicans have been rightfully critical of the iron-handed, closed process of the House Democratic leadership. Will the Democratic minority have a chance for their voices to be heard and votes to take place on their issues—yes. Will it happen on their timetable—no. The first one hundred days of the 104th Congress will be dedicated solely to fulfilling the *Contract* with the American people.

# Appendix

The following Republican candidates, listed by name, state, and Congressional district, signed the Contract with America on the steps of the U.S. Capitol on September 27, 1994. An asterisk indicates those men and women elected on November 8, 1994, to serve in the U.S. House of Representatives. Their pledge: "If we break this Contract, throw us out."

Sonny Callahan, Alabama, 1*
Terry Everett, Alabama, 2*
Wayne Parker, Jr., Alabama, 5
Spencer Bachus, Alabama, 6*
Alfred Middleton, Sr., Alabama, 7
Matt Salmon, Arizona, 1*
Robert McDonald, Arizona, 2
Bob Stump, Arizona, 3*
John Shaddegg, Arizona, 4*
Jim Kolbe, Arizona, 5*
J.D. Hayworth, Arizona, 6*
Warren Dupwe, Arkansas, 1
Bill Powell, Arkansas, 2
Tim Hutchinson, Arkansas, 3*
Jay Dickey, Arkansas, 4*
Frank Riggs, California, 1*
Wally Herger, California, 2*
Tim LeFever, California, 3
John Doolittle, California, 4*
Robert Dinsmore, California, 5
Mike Nugent, California, 6
Charles Hughes, California, 7

Elsa Cheung, California, 8
Bill Baker, California, 10*
Richard Pombo, California, 11*
Deborah Wilder, California, 12
Ben Brink, California, 14
Lyle Smith, California, 16
George Radanovich, California, 19*
Bill Thomas, California, 21*
Andrea Seastrand, California, 22*
Elton Gallegly, California, 23*
Richard Sybert, California, 24
Howard McKeon, California, 25*
Carlos Moorhead, California, 27*
David Dreier, California, 28*
Paul Stepanek, California, 29
John Flores, California, 31
Ernie Farhat, California, 32
Albert Nunez, California, 34
Susan Brooks, California, 36*
Steve Horn, California, 38*
Ed Royce, California, 39*
Jerry Lewis, California, 40*
Jay Kim, California, 41*
Robert Guzman, California, 42
Ken Calvert, California, 43*
Sonny Bono, California, 44*
Dana Rohrabacher, California, 45*
Robert Dornan, California, 46*
Christopher Cox, California, 47*
Ron Packard, California, 48*
Brian Bilbray, California, 49*
Mary Alice Acevedo, California, 50

Randy Cunningham, California, 51*
Duncan Hunter, California, 52*
Pat Miller, Colorado, 2
Scott McInnis, Colorado, 3*
Wayne Allard, Colorado, 4*
Joel Hefley, Colorado, 5*
Dan Schaefer, Colorado, 6*
Douglas Putnam, Connecticut, 1
Ed Munster, Connecticut, 2
Christopher Shays, Connecticut, 4*
Gary Franks, Connecticut, 5*
Nancy Johnson, Connecticut, 6*
Michael Castle, Delaware, At Large
Joe Scarborough, Florida, 1*
Carole Griffin, Florida, 2
Marc Little, Florida, 3
Tillie Fowler, Florida, 4*
Don Garlits, Florida, 5
Cliff Stearns, Florida, 6*
John Mica, Florida, 7*
Bill McCollum, Florida, 8*
Michael Bilirakis, Florida, 9*
Bill Young, Florida, 10*
Mark Sharpe, Florida, 11
Charles Canady, Florida, 12*
Dan Miller, Florida, 13*
Porter Goss, Florida, 14*
Dave Weldon, Florida, 15*
Mark Foley, Florida, 16*
Peter Tsakanikas, Florida, 19
Bevery Kennedy, Florida, 20
Clay Shaw, Florida, 22*

Jack Kingston, Georgia, 1*
Mac Collins, Georgia, 3*
John Linder, Georgia, 4*
Dale Dixon, Georgia, 5
Newt Gingrich, Georgia, 6*
Bob Barr, Georgia, 7*
Saxby Chambliss, Georgia, 8*
Charles Norwood, Georgia, 10*
Woodrow Lovett, Georgia, 11
Orson Swindle, Hawaii, 1
Helen Chenoweth, Idaho, 1*
Mike Crapo, Idaho, 2*
Jim Nalepa, Illinois, 3
Steven Valtierra, Illinois, 4
Mike Flanagan, Illinois, 5*
Henry Hyde, Illinois, 6*
Phillip Crane, Illinois, 8*
George Larney, Illinois, 9
John Porter, Illinois, 10*
Jerry Weller, Illinois, 11*
Harris Fawell, Illinois, 13*
Dennis Hastert, Illinois, 14*
Tom Ewing, Illinois, 15*
Don Manzullo, Illinois, 16*
Jim Anderson, Illinois, 17
Brent Winters, Illinois, 19
Bill Owens, Illinois, 20
John Larson, Indiana, 1
David McIntosh, Indiana, 2*
Richard Burkett, Indiana, 3
Mark Souder, Indiana, 4*
Steve Buyer, Indiana, 5*

Dan Burton, Indiana, 6*
John Myers, Indiana, 7*
John Hostetler, Indiana, 8*
Jean Leising, Indiana, 9
Marvin Scott, Indiana, 10
Jim Leach, Iowa, 1*
Jim Nussle, Iowa, 2*
Jim Lightfoot, Iowa, 3*
Greg Ganske, Iowa, 4*
Tom Latham, Iowa, 5*
Pat Roberts, Kansas, 1*
Jan Meyers, Kansas, 3*
Todd Tiahrt, Kansas, 4*
Edward Whitfield, Kentucky, 1*
Ron Lewis, Kentucky, 2*
Susan Stokes, Kentucky, 3
Jim Bunning, Kentucky, 4*
Harold Rogers, Kentucky, 5*
Matthew Wills, Kentucky, 6
Bob Livingston, Louisiana, 1*
Jim McCrery, Louisiana, 5*
Richard Baker, Louisiana, 6*
Jim Longley, Jr., Maine, 1*
Richard Bennett, Maine, 2
Wayne Gilchrest, Maryland, 1*
Bob Ehrlich, Maryland, 2*
Robert Ryan Tousey, Maryland, 3
Michele Dyson, Maryland, 4
Don Devine, Maryland, 5
Roscoe Bartlett, Maryland, 6*
Kenneth Kondner, Maryland, 7
Connie Morella, Maryland, 8*

Peter Blute, Massachusetts, 3*
Dave Coleman, Massachusetts, 5
Peter Torkildsen, Massachusetts, 6*
Brad Bailey, Massachusetts, 7
Michael Murphy, Massachusetts, 9
Keith Hemeon, Massachusetts, 10
Gil Ziegler, Michigan, 1
Peter Hoekstra, Michigan, 2*
Vern Ehlers, Michigan, 3*
Dave Camp, Michigan, 4*
William Anderson, Michigan, 5
Fred Upton, Michigan, 6*
Nick Smith, Michigan, 7*
Dick Chrysler, Michigan, 8*
Megan O'Neill, Michigan, 9
Donald Lobsinger, Michigan, 10
Joe Knollenberg, Michigan, 11*
John Pappageorge, Michigan, 12
John Schall, Michigan, 13
Ken Larkin, Michigan, 16
Gil Gutknecht, Minnesota, 1*
Gary Revier, Minnesota, 2
James Ramstad, Minnesota, 3*
Dennis Newinski, Minnesota, 4
Tad Jude, Minnesota, 6
Bernie Omann, Minnesota, 7
Roger Wicker, Mississippi, 1*
Bill Jordan, Mississippi, 2
Dutch Dabbs, Mississippi, 3
Mike Wood, Mississippi, 4
George Barlos, Mississippi, 5
Donald Counts, Missouri, 1

Jim Talent, Missouri, 2*
Gary Gill, Missouri, 3
James Noland, Jr., Missouri, 4
Ron Freeman, Missouri, 5
Tina Tucker, Missouri, 6
Mel Hancock, Missouri, 7*
Bill Emerson, Missouri, 8*
Kenny Hulshof, Missouri, 9*
Doug Bereuter, Nebraska, 1*
Jon Christensen, Nebraska, 2*
Bill Barrett, Nebraska, 3*
John Ensign, Nevada, 1*
Barbara Vucanovich, Nevada, 2*
Bill Zeliff, New Hampshire, 1*
Charles Bass, New Hampshire, 2*
James Hogan, New Jersey, 1
Frank LoBiondo, New Jersey, 2*
Jim Saxton, New Jersey, 3*
Chris Smith, New Jersey, 4*
Marge Roukema, New Jersey, 5*
Mike Herson, New Jersey, 6
Bob Franks, New Jersey, 7*
William Martini, New Jersey, 8*
Jim Ford, New Jersey, 10
Rodney Frelinghuysen, New Jersey, 11*
Richard Zimmer, New Jersey, 12*
Steven Schiff, New Mexico, 1*
Joseph Skeen, New Mexico, 2*
Gregg Bemis, Jr., New Mexico, 3
Michael Forbes, New York, 1*
Rick Lazio, New York, 2*
Peter King, New York, 3*

Daniel Frisa, New York, 4*

Grant Lally, New York, 5

David Askren, New York, 8

James McCall, New York, 9

Susan Molinari, New York, 13*

Andrew Hartzell, Jr., New York, 18

Sue Kelly, New York, 19*

Benjamin Gilman, New York, 20*

Joseph Gomez, New York, 21

Gerald Solomon, New York, 22*

Sherwood Boehlert, New York, 23*

John McHugh, New York, 24*

James Walsh, New York, 25*

Bob Moppert, New York, 26

Bill Paxon, New York, 27*

Renee Davison, New York, 28

Bill Miller, New York, 29

Jack Quinn, New York, 30*

Amory Houghton, New York, 31*

Ted Tyler, North Carolina, 1

David Funderburk, North Carolina, 2*

Walter Jones, Jr., North Carolina, 3*

Fred Heineman, North Carolina, 4*

Richard Burr, North Carolina, 5*

Howard Coble, North Carolina, 6*

Robert Anderson, North Carolina, 7

Sherill Morgan, North Carolina, 8

Sue Myrick, North Carolina, 9*

Cass Ballenger, North Carolina, 10*

Charles Taylor, North Carolina, 11*

Gary Porter, North Dakota, At Large

Steve Chabot, Ohio, 1*

Robert Portman, Ohio, 2*

Dave Westbrock, Ohio, 3

Michael Oxley, Ohio, 4*

Paul Gillmor, Ohio, 5*

Frank Cremeans, Ohio, 6*

David Hobson, Ohio, 7*

John Boehner, Ohio, 8*

Randy Whitman, Ohio, 9

Martin Hoke, Ohio, 10*

John Kasich, Ohio, 12*

Greg White, Ohio, 13

Lynn Slaby, Ohio, 14

Deborah Pryce, Ohio, 15*

Ralph Regula, Ohio, 16*

Mike Meister, Ohio, 17

Robert Ney, Ohio, 18*

Steven LaTourette, Ohio, 19*

Steve Largent, Oklahoma, 1*

J.C. Watts, Oklahoma, 4*

Ernest Istook, Oklahoma, 5*

Frank Lucas, Oklahoma, 6*

Bill Witt, Oregon, 1

Wes Cooley, Oregon, 2*

John Newkirk, Oregon, 4

Roger Gordon, Pennsylvania, 1

Lawrence Watson, Pennsylvania, 2

Ed Peglow, Pennsylvania, 4

Bill Clinger, Pennsylvania, 5*

Frederick Levering, Pennsylvania, 6

Curt Weldon, Pennsylvania, 7*

James Greenwood, Pennsylvania, 8*

Bud Shuster, Pennsylvania, 9*

Joe McDade, Pennsylvania, 10*

Jurij Podolak, Pennsylvania, 11

Bill Choby, Pennsylvania, 12

Jon Fox, Pennsylvania, 13*

John Clark, Pennsylvania, 14

Robert Walker, Pennsylvania, 16*

George Gekas, Pennsylvania, 17*

John McCarty, Pennsylvania, 18

William Goodling, Pennsylvania, 19*

Mike McCormick, Pennsylvania, 20

Philip English, Pennsylvania, 21*

Kevin Vigilante, Rhode Island, 1

John Elliot, Rhode Island, 2

Amata Coleman Radewagen, Samoa, At Large

Mark Sanford, South Carolina, 1*

Floyd Spence, South Carolina, 2*

Lindsey Graham, South Carolina, 3*

Bob Inglis, South Carolina, 4*

Larry Bigham, South Carolina, 5

Gary McLeod, South Carolina, 6

Jan Berkhout, South Dakota, At Large

James Quillen, Tennessee, 1*

John Duncan, Tennessee, 2*

Zach Wamp, Tennessee, 3*

Van Hilleary, Tennessee, 4*

John Osborne, Tennessee, 5

Steve Gill, Tennessee, 6

Ed Bryant, Tennessee, 7*

Rod DeBerry, Tennessee, 9

Michael Blankenship, Texas, 1

Donna Peterson, Texas, 2

Sam Johnson, Texas, 3*

David Bridges, Texas, 4
Pete Sessions, Texas, 5
Joe Barton, Texas, 6*
William Archer, Texas, 7*
Jack Fields, Texas, 8*
Steve Stockman, Texas, 9*
Jo Baylor, Texas, 10
Jim Broyles, Texas, 11
Ernest Anderson, Jr., Texas, 12
William Thornberry, Texas, 13*
Jim Deats, Texas, 14
Tom Haughey, Texas, 15
Bobby Ortiz, Texas, 16
Phil Boone, Texas, 17
Jerry Burley, Texas, 18
Larry Combest, Texas, 19*
Carl Colyer, Texas, 20
Lamar Smith, Texas, 21*
Tom DeLay, Texas, 22*
Henry Bonilla, Texas, 23*
Gene Fontenot, Texas, 25
Dick Armey, Texas, 26*
Erol Stone, Texas, 27
David Slatter, Texas, 28
James Hansen, Utah, 1*
Enid Greene Waldholtz, Utah, 2*
Dixie Thompson, Utah, 3
Herb Bateman, Virginia, 1*
Jim Chapman, Virginia, 2
Tom Ward, Virginia, 3
George Sweet III, Virginia, 4
George Landrith III, Virginia, 5

Bob Goodlatte, Virginia, 6*
Thomas Bliley, Virginia, 7*
Kyle McSlarrow, Virginia, 8
Steve Fast, Virginia, 9
Frank Wolf, Virginia, 10*
Tom Davis, Virginia, 11*
Rick White, Washington, 1*
Jack Metcalf, Washington, 2*
Linda Smith, Washington, 3*
Richard Hastings, Washington, 4*
George Nethercutt, Washington, 5*
Jennifer Dunn, Washington, 8*
Randy Tate, Washington, 9*
Samuel Cravotta, West Virginia, 2
Ben Waldman, West Virginia, 3
Mark Neumann, Wisconsin, 1*
Scott Klug, Wisconsin, 2*
Steve Gunderson, Wisconsin, 3*
Tom Reynolds, Wisconsin, 4
Stephen Hollingshead, Wisconsin, 5
Thomas Petri, Wisconsin, 6*
Scott West, Wisconsin, 7
Toby Roth, Wisconsin, 8*
Jim Sensenbrenner, Wisconsin, 9*
Barbara Cubin, Wyoming, At Large*

# Rep. Newt Gingrich
## Washington Research Group Symposium
## Washington, D.C.
### *November 11, 1994*

---

SEVENTY-SIX YEARS today the armistice was declared at the eleventh hour of the eleventh day of the eleventh month in what was then called the Great War. Indirectly, that had an enormous impact on my life because it was while my dad was stationed with the Army in Europe and I was a fourteen-year-old freshman in high school that we went to the battlefield in Verdun, which was the largest battlefield in the Western front of that war. We spent a weekend with a friend of his who had been on a death march in the Philippines and served three years in a Japanese prison camp. The Great War was both an example of what happens when leadership fails and societies collide and it was an example in its aftermath of what happens when people lie to themselves about the objective realities of the human condition. Because instead of leading to world peace as Woodrow Wilson had so devoutly hoped, it, in fact, ultimately led to the Second World War. And instead of leading to greater freedom for all human beings, as Woodrow Wilson's Fourteen Points had hoped, it led to Nazism and the Soviet empire, the Gulag, and Auschwitz.

And so it is both good for us today to remember the cost paid by those who believe enough in freedom to have died for it and useful to remind ourselves that that price has to be paid every year and every week and that it is better by far to pay that price in peace-time by being vigilant and by trying to do that which is right than it is to allow your society to decay or to have inadequate leadership and drift into a cataclysm comparable to the First and Second World Wars.

And that's not just a foreign policy or national defense battle cry. What is ultimately at stake in our current environment is literally the future of American civilization as it has existed for the last several hundred years. I'm a history teacher by background, and I would assert and defend on any campus in this country that it is impossible to maintain civilization with twelve-year-olds having babies, with fifteen-year-olds killing each other, with seventeen-year-olds dying of AIDS, and with eighteen-year-olds ending up with diplomas they can't even read. What is at issue is literally not Republican or Democrat or liberal or conservative, but the question of whether or not our civilization will survive.

Since the election, the article which has most accurately captured its essence is Charles Krauthammer's column this morning in *The Washington Post*, which makes the correct point that you have the most explicitly ideologically committed House Republican Party in modern history. That we held an event on September 27 on the Capitol steps that over 300 members signed or candidates signed up for. That we told the country in a full-page ad in *TV Guide* where we were going and the direction we would take. That President Clinton and Tony Coelho took up the challenge. That the Democratic National Committee ran $2 million of ads attacking the *Contract with America*. That the President personally attacked the *Contract* virtually everywhere he went. And that in the end there was the most shatteringly one-sided Republican victory since 1946.

Since then, there's been an enormous effort by the Washington elite to avoid the reality that this lesson was actually about some fairly big ideas—Which direction do you want to go in?—and that those who argued for counterculture values, bigger government, redistributionist economics, and bureaucracies deciding how you should spend your money, were on the losing end in virtually every part of the country.

When in Georgia we elect five statewide elected officials, we have a majority seven to four in the House delegation, there may be something that's a message. And you can either say, well, but that's those southern Christian religious groups. Fine. In Washington state we went from seven to one Democrat to six to two Republican. You can hardly argue that it's Southern fundamentalism that swept Washington state. And yet I've seen talk shows where learned experts who were totally wrong a week ago are equally wrong now. It's amazing how often we can watch experts who had no idea what was about to happen explain to us afterwards what it meant. Part of the problem is stereotyping.

Let me discuss several stereotypes that I think are very important—or several things that break out of the stereotype. Part of our problem is the level at which we think. I use a planning model and a leadership model that is very explicit. The planning model is derived from how George Marshall and Dwight Eisenhower and Franklin Roosevelt managed the Second World War, which was the most complex, large human activity ever undertaken. Essentially, they had a four-layer model, and it's a hierarchy. The top of it was vision, and after you understood your vision of what you're doing you designed strategies, and once you have your vision and strategies clear you designed projects which were the building blocks of your strategies, and inside the context of those projects you delegated dramatically an entrepreneurial model in which a project was a definable, delegatable achievement. Eisenhower's job was to invade the continent of Europe, defeat the German army and occupy the German heartland. His actual order from the combined chiefs was two paragraphs, all the rest was detail. That's delegation on a fairly grand scale.

At the bottom of the model is tactics, what you do every day. Washington, D.C., is a city so consumed by its own tactical self-amusement that it's very hard for the city to have any sense of projects, and the concept of vision and strategies is almost beyond its comprehension.

The second model is a leadership model that is a process. That is they're not a hierarchy, all the words that define this model are equally important, but there's a sequence that matters. It's a very direct sequence: Listen, learn, help, and lead. You listen to the American people, you learn from the American people, you help the American people; and in a rational society, if people know you'll listen to them, learn from them and help them, they want you to lead them.

So the job of a leader is first of all to think about things, develop a vision and strategies and projects and tactics, and then go back out and listen to the people and find out whether or not in fact they're on the same wavelength. And if not, to assume that there's at least a better than even chance that it is the people and not the elite who are right.

That's a very specific model. You may disagree with it or not like it but it's a very specific model and if you want to understand what the next Speaker of the House is going to function like, it's a model that will in fact be fairly predictive.

It's very hard for the Washington elite to come to grips with the reality that there's now a national Republican Party. That's the biggest single message of this election. That for the first time in history, the civil war, in effect, is over, and Republicans were able to run everywhere simultaneously. And, standing on Ronald Reagan's shoulders, the Republican Party now has enough recruits and enough resources and enough leaders to actually be capable of running everywhere. And it was literally the first election in history where there were fewer Democrats without opposition than Republicans. We had more Republicans running unopposed for the House in 1994 than there were Democrats. That has never, ever, in the history of the two parties, for 140 years, been true. And, we won, which makes it even more historic.

This was clearly a historic election which clearly had a mandate. And that's outside the Washington elite's view, and they don't want to believe that because it's not the mandate they wanted.

I want to draw a distinction between two words, because we're going to get into a lot of confusion at the vision level about these two words. I am very prepared to cooperate with the Clinton administration. I am not prepared to compromise. The two words are very different. On everything on which we can find agreement, I will cooperate.

On those things that are at the core of our *Contract*, those things which are at the core of our philosophy, and on those things where we believe we represent the vast majority of Americans, there will be no compromise. So let me draw the distinction: Cooperation, yes; compromise, no.

People have been trying to figure out how to put me in a box, and it's very hard because I don't fit boxes very well. The best description of me is that I'm a conservative futurist. For a long time, I have been friends with Alvin and Heidi Toffler, the authors of *Future Shock* and *The Third Way*. I really believe it's useful to think about the twenty-first century. On the other hand, I believe the most powerful single doctrine for the leadership of human beings and for their opportunity to pursue happiness is the *Federalist Papers,* Tocqueville's *Democracy in America*, the Declaration of Independence, and the Constitution. I also recommend to all the congressional staffs that they buy Peter Drucker's *Effective Executive*, study W. Edwards Deming's concepts of quality, look at the new Progress and Freedom Foundation's report on Alvin Toffler's works. I also suggest immersing yourself in the Founding Fathers. These people thought a long time about the nature of being human, about the problems of power, about how to organize a free society so it could sustain freedom. And if you can combine the two, you can begin to create an opportunity for every American to participate in ways that will prove to be quite remarkable.

Now, that obviously doesn't fit anybody's current word processor. We want to get to the twenty-first century, and we want to do so in a way that's effective.

There are five large changes we have to go through. First, we have to accelerate the transition from a second wave mechanical, bureaucratic society to a third wave information society, to use Alvin Toffler's model. Two simple examples: One, imagine the speed and ease with which you use a bank teller card anywhere on the planet and electronically verify your account and get money; second, imagine what happens when you call the federal government about a case. There's no objective reason that institutions of government have to be two or three generations behind the curve in information systems and management, but they are. And that means, for example, if we're really serious about distance medicine and about distance learning and about distance work, we could revolutionize the quality of life in rural America and create the greatest explosion of new opportunity for rural America in history. And yet, we're currently moving in the opposite direction so that at a time when the IRS should be making it easier to have a home office, they make it harder. Now that's foolish. It's exactly the wrong direction.

Second, we will change the rules of the House to require that all documents and all conference reports and all committee reports be filed electronically as well as in writing and that they cannot be filed until they are available to any citizen who wants to pull them up. Thus, information will be available to every citizen in the country at the same moment that it is available to the highest paid Washington lobbyist. Over time, that will change the entire flow of information and the entire quality of knowledge in the country and it will change the way people will try to play games in the legislative process.

Third, we need to recognize the objective reality of the world market, to realize that we create American jobs through world sales and that we need to make a conscious national decision that we want to have the highest value added jobs on the planet with the greatest productivity so we can have the highest take-home pay and the greatest range of choices in lifestyles. In order to do that we have to literally rethink the assumptions that grew up in a self-indulgent national economy and we have to recognize that litigation, taxation, regulation, welfare, education, the very structure of government, the structure of health—all those things have to be reexamined from the standpoint of what will make us the most competitive society on the planet, the most desirable place to invest to create jobs, and the place with the best trained and most entrepreneurial work force, most committed to Deming's concepts of quality.

That's a big challenge. One step, frankly, has to be that every child in America should be required to do at least two hours of homework a night or they're being cheated for the rest of their lives in their ability to compete with the Germans and the Japanese and the Chinese. Now, one of the differences I would suggest between where we are going and where our friends on the left would go, is I do not derive from that a belief that we need a federal department of home-work checkers. I believe that we should say to every parent in the country, "Your child ought to be doing two hours of homework. If they're not, go see the teacher. If you can't convince the teacher, get a bet-ter teacher, and in the interim assign it yourself." I was taught to read by my grandmother. General George Marshall was taught to read by his aunt. The objec-tive fact is, historically this was a country that got the job done, not a country that found scapegoats for fail-ure. And so we've simply got to reassert a level of civic responsibility we're not used to.

Fourth, we have to replace the welfare state with an opportunity society. It is impossible to take the Great Society structure of bureaucracy, the redistri-butionist model of how wealth is acquired, and the counterculture value system that now permeates the way we deal with the poor, and have any hope of fix-ing them. They are a disaster. They ruin the poor, they create a culture of poverty and a culture of violence which is destructive of this civilization, and they have to be replaced thoroughly from the ground up.

This should be done in cooperation with the poor. The people who have the most to gain from elimi-nating the culture of poverty and replacing it with a culture of productivity are the people currently trapped in a nightmare, living in public housing projects with no one going to work, living in neighborhoods with no physical safety, their children forced to walk into buildings where there will be no learning, and living in a community where taxes and red tape and regulation destroy their hope of creating new entrepreneurial small businesses and doing what every other generation of poor Americans have done, which is to leave poverty behind by acquiring productivity.

We simply need to reach out and erase the slate and start over, and we need to start with the premise that every American is endowed by their Creator with certain inalienable rights, among which are life, liberty, and the pursuit of happiness, and that extends to the poorest child in Washington, D.C., and the poorest child in West Virginia, and the poorest child in American Indian reservations. And we have been failing all of them because we have lacked the courage to be mentally tough enough to get the job done. I think it can be done, but I think it's very deep and represents a very bold change.

We have to recognize that American exceptionalism—to use Everett Carl Ladd's phrase—is real; that this has been the most successful civilization in the history of the human race at liberating people to pursue happiness. There is no other society in history where as many people from as many cultures speaking as many languages could come together and become a nation, and where they could then be liberated to go off and be who they wanted to be. This is a country where Colin Powell and John Shalikashvili can both be chairman of the Joint Chiefs and nobody

even thinks about the remarkable difference in eth-
nicity because they're Americans, and that's the way
it should be.

That means we have to say to the counterculture:
Nice try, you failed, you're wrong. And we have to
simply, calmly, methodically reassert American civilization and reestablish the conditions, which I believe
starts with the work ethic. You cannot study 300 years
of American civilization without coming to the con-
clusion that working and being expected to work and
being involved—and work may be for money or it may
be at home, it may be a hobby that you pursue, but
the sense of energy, the pursuit of happiness, which
is not—it's an active verb—not happiness stamps, not
a department of happiness, not therapy for happiness.
Pursuit. This is also a muscular society and we've been
kidding ourselves about it. The New Hampshire slo-
gan is "Live free or die." It is not "Live free or whine."
And so we have to think through what are the deeper
underlying cultural meanings of being American and
how do we reassert them.

Fifth, and lastly, and this is one where I, frankly,
became more radical all fall. I realized as I would talk
to audiences—I was in 127 districts in the last two
years, and I realized as I would talk to audiences that
there was an enormous danger that they were going
to say, "Terrific speech, let's elect Gingrich Speaker,
let's elect our local candidate to the House, they'll do
the job." And let me tell all of you flatly, the long
experiment in professional politicians and professional
government is over, and it failed. You cannot hire a
teacher to teach your child and walk off and then blame

the teacher. You cannot hire a policeman to protect your neighborhood and then walk off and blame the police. You cannot hire a public health service to protect your health and then walk off and blame the public health service.

We have to reestablish—and I particularly want to thank Gordon Wood, who will probably get in a lot of trouble at Brown University for my using his name, but Gordon Wood's understanding of the origins of the American Revolution and his understanding of the core intent of Jeffersonian politics was for me a liberating moment because it's his argument that what Jefferson understood was that you had to have limited but effective government precisely in order to liberate people to engage in civic responsibility, and that the larger government grew, the more you would crowd out civic responsibility.

Now, this means that my challenge to the American people is simple. You really want to dramatically reduce power in Washington? You have to be willing to take more responsibility back home. You really want to reduce the bureaucracy of the welfare state? You have to accept greater responsibility back home. We are going to have to be partners. This is going to have to be a team in which we work together to renew American civilization, which is frankly why I teach the course I do on videotape and we make it available across the country. In fact, I will shamelessly tell you we use an 800 number. I hope all of you will call. And I'm very serious about it. I mean, if you're not going to take the time to learn about ideas, why should you think we'll change? The things that are wrong in America are not wrong because of money or lack of money; they're wrong because we've had a bad set of ideas that haven't worked and we need to replace them with a good set of ideas. And you can actually call. It's 1-800-TO RENEW—T-O-R-E-N-E-W.

The event on September 27 was designed as a sub-set of these big principles. The Capitol steps event basically said, Look, we are a team, we are going to go in a dramatically different direction, we're going to give you eight reforms on the opening day, starting with the Shays Act, which will apply to the Congress every law it applies to the rest of the country so congressmen will learn all the problems they've imposed on everybody else.

We are going to cut the number of congressional committee staffs by a third, and we sent a letter to that effect to Speaker Tom Foley on Wednesday, frankly in order to allow the Democratic staff to know that a substantial number of them ought to be looking for jobs, because we thought that was the most decent and most correct way to deal with it. We are going to cut the number of congressional committees. We are going to eliminate the current services budget and replace it with a straight line budget, where if you have a dollar increase it counts as a dollar increase. This is the only place in the world where you can increase spending massively and it counts as a cut. And it has been a major source of the problem of dealing with the deficit because you create a linguistic barrier to honesty. And so we're simply going to eliminate it. You're not going to get a current services budget in this Congress—not on the House side.

Now, at the end of the opening day, we will introduce the ten bills we described in the *Contract*. We will read the *Contract* as the opening item of business every day for the first hundred days, and at the end of the first hundred days the American people, at Easter, will be able to say they saw a group of people who actually said what they were going to do and then kept their word. Now, we don't guarantee we'll pass all ten, and it's very clear in the *Contract* that what—some of these are very controversial—litigation reform, including malpractice, product liability and strike law firms is one item; a balanced budget amendment to the Constitution; a vote on term limits; an effective, enforceable death penalty with a one-time unified appeal; beginning to phase-out the marriage penalty in the tax code; allowing senior citizens to earn up to $39,000 a year without penalty from Social Security; a capital gains cut and indexing. These are not small things, but they move in the right direction. Welfare reform, emphasizing work and family. A line-item veto, including frankly, a line-item veto for this President, so that we as Republican conservatives are prepared to give to President Clinton a line-item veto because we think it's right for America. These are real changes. It's going to be real hard to do and it's going to take a lot of people helping.

Let me say one last thing: If this just degenerates after an historic election back into the usual baloney of politics in Washington and pettiness in Washington, then the American people I believe will move toward a third party in a massive way. I think they are fed up with Washington, they are fed up with its games, they are fed up with petty partisanship. I don't think they mind grand partisanship, and there's a big difference. To have a profound disagreement over the direction of your country or over the principles by which your economy works, or over the manner in which your government should structure resources, that is legitimate and the American people believe in that level of debate and relish it.

The question will be over the next six months, can we reach out to the American people, can we recruit enough of them—notice I didn't say "Republicans"— the American people. Can we reach out to enough Democrats? Jack Kemp had a very encouraging talk with a leading member of the Black Caucus about working together and developing a program that is very bold and very dramatic in terms of helping the poor create jobs and helping those who want to rise have a real opportunity to acquire wealth and to create a better future for themselves. Now, if we can reach out and truly try to do this—and remember what I quoted on the Capitol steps, which was Franklin Delano Roosevelt, on March 4, 1933, standing in his braces at a time when it was inconceivable that somebody who had polio could be elected to major office, and standing there and saying on a wintry, overcast day in the middle of the Great Depression that we had nothing to fear but fear itself.

When you hear gunshots in your nation's capital at night and you know that young Americans have died needlessly, then I would suggest to you that we have every reason to have the moral courage to confront every weakness of the current structure and to replace it, and if the first wave of experiments fail, to have the courage to say, "Well, that one didn't work," and have a second one and a third one and a fourth one. And the Monday morning we wake up and we can look on the morning news and no young American was killed anywhere in America, and we can know that every one of them is going to a school where they're actually learning how to read, and we know that they live under a tax code where if they want to it's easy to start creating jobs and to have your own business, and it's easy to start accumulating a little money to create a better future, that morning I think we can say, "Okay, this journey has been worth it." But until that day, it just stays politics.

We have an enormous amount of work to do. All I can promise you on the side of the House Republicans is that we're going to be open to working with everyone, that we will cooperate with anyone, and we will compromise with no one, and that's the base of where we're going and that's what we believe this election is all about.

# ABOUT THE EDITORS

ED GILLESPIE is the policy and communications director of the House Republican Conference. A graduate of the Catholic University of America, he has worked for Rep. Dick Armey of Texas since 1985. He lives with his wife, Cathy, son, John Patrick, and daughter, Carrie, in Alexandria, Virginia.

BOB SCHELLHAS was deputy director of the *Contract with America* project at the Republican National Committee. A campaign manager, political advisor, and field organizer for seven statewide and Congressional campaigns in Iowa, Michigan, and Nebraska, he has served as a legislative assistant and communications director to Rep. Dave Camp of Michigan, and to former Rep. Bill Schuette of Michigan. A graduate of Central Michigan University, he lives in Washington, D.C.